CLASSIC BASEBALL

CLASSIC BASEBALL

Timeless Tales,
Immortal Moments

JOHN ROSENGREN

ROWMAN & LITTLEFIELD
Lanham • Boulder • New York • London

Published by Rowman & Littlefield
An imprint of The Rowman & Littlefield Publishing Group, Inc.
4501 Forbes Boulevard, Suite 200, Lanham, Maryland 20706
www.rowman.com

6 Tinworth Street, London, SE11 5AL, United Kingdom

British Library Cataloguing in Publication Information Available

Library of Congress Cataloging-in-Publication Data

Names: Rosengren, John, author.
Title: Classic baseball : timeless tales, immortal moments / John
   Rosengren.
Description: Lanham, Maryland : Rowman & Littlefield, [2022] | Summary:
   "This collection of timeless baseball stories can be read again and
   again for its poignancy, humor, and celebration of the national pastime,
   whether it be John Roseboro forgiving Juan Marichal for clubbing him in
   the head with a bat, Elston Howard integrating the Yankees, or baseball
   played on snowshoes in a remote Wisconsin town"—Provided by publisher.
Identifiers: LCCN 2021026100 (print) | LCCN 2021026101 (ebook) | ISBN
   9781538156964 (cloth) | ISBN 9781538156971 (epub)
Subjects: LCSH: Baseball—United States—Anecdotes.
Classification: LCC GV873 .R67 2022 (print) | LCC GV873 (ebook) | DDC
   796.3570973—dc23
LC record available at https://lccn.loc.gov/2021026100
LC ebook record available at https://lccn.loc.gov/2021026101

For my home team
Maria, Alison, and Brendan

CONTENTS

INTRODUCTION

One of the many things I love about baseball is how the lulls in the action allow an elder to pass along explanations, history, and lore about the game. For me, that elder was my father, who took me to Twins games at Met Stadium in the 1970s. Throughout my formative years, he told me the same stories, over and over: how he sat on the warning track with other kids at Nicollet Park to watch the Minneapolis Millers for only a dime and a Wheaties box top; the way Millers future Hall of Fame third baseman Ray Dandridge fielded a hard-hit grounder but waited until the last second to rifle a throw that nailed the runner out at the last instant; or the time my dad took the train to Chicago to see his boyhood hero Ted Williams hit a home run at Comiskey. I never tired of those stories.

Baseball—rooted as it is in tradition and nostalgia—lends itself to the retelling of its timeless stories. So it is with the stories in this collection. Each is a slice of a moment or character or aspect of baseball that can be enjoyed more than once.

I come at the game from many angles: a fan, an umpire, a player, a coach, and a member of the Society for American Baseball Research. Those different vantage points have given me an appreciation for the richness, variety, and complexity of the game. I especially treasure hearing—and being able to tell—stories that reflect those various angles.

It is in my capacity as a journalist and author that I have learned the most about the game—and discovered the stories it has to tell us. During the course of more than three decades, I've had the good fortune to be able to meet some of the game's greats—Hank Aaron, Rod Carew, Orlando Cepeda, Bob Feller, Harmon Killebrew, Ralph Kiner, Juan Marichal, Willie Mays, Frank Robinson, and Dave Winfield. I've also had the chance to talk to some of the game's more colorful players, people like Jim Bouton and Bill Lee. These articles, which originally appeared in such publications as *VICE Sports*, the *New Yorker*, and *Sports Illustrated*, feature some of their stories. They also feature tales about Josh Gibson, Branch Rickey, Harvey Haddix, and other legends of the game, along with entertaining tales about some of baseball's equally compelling but lesser-known personalities (meet Mark Hamburger and Willians Astudillo).

The articles here go behind the scenes of some of the game's bigger moments: How *did* Sandy Koufax spend Yom Kippur the day he famously did not pitch the first game of the 1965 World Series? Why did it take the Yankees so long to integrate America's team? What prompted Juan Marichal to club John Roseboro over the head with his bat—and how did the two ever become friends? How was it that Ty Cobb made it out alive but Christy Mathewson eventually succumbed to the effects of a chemical warfare training drill gone wrong during World War I?

There are also stories here—equally rich in baseball essence—that you've likely never heard: the one about the game played by the all-Black Monrovians against the local chapter of the Ku Klux Klan. An account of baseball played on snowshoes deep in the Wisconsin woods during summertime. The 1945 GI World Series held in the Hitler Youth Stadium in Nuremberg where Hitler had preached his bombastic propaganda. A fan on a quest to see Alex Rodriguez notch his 3,000th hit. The baseball museum that claims as part of its collection a hot dog half eaten by Babe Ruth. And so on.

There's something for everyone, whether you're one of those fans who stayed loyal to the Cubs during their long championship drought or a casual follower of your local team. Whether you come from a red or blue state. Whether you like the designated-hitter rule or not. Baseball connects us, gives us common ground. Quick story to illustrate: During the 1987 World Series, my hometown Minnesota Twins sparked the possibility of not only winning their first World Series, but also giving the state its first championship in a major sport since 1954, won by the Lakers before they abandoned us for Los Angeles. The excitement that swept the state wholesale was nowhere more evident to me than the morning after the Twins won Game Two to take a 2–0 lead and a Hmong woman at the bus stop gushed in broken English praise for the team.

Another quick story, this one from grad school: The director of the creative writing program at Boston University, Leslie Epstein, was notoriously hard on students with his comments about our short stories. We often sought solace from his stinging criticism after class in the pub across the street from our classroom, where we licked our wounds and tried to bolster our sagging egos. Throughout my time in the program, Leslie only liked one of the six stories I submitted, a baseball tale about a farm kid who led the league in getting hit by pitches. Although I should have suspected it at the time, it wasn't until eight years later that I discovered his deep love of baseball when his son Theo was hired to run the Red Sox. In the years since, Leslie and I have enjoyed many good discussions about the game and—God bless him—he has supported me in my writing career.

Back to my dad, he passed away in 2006. I wish he were still around to be able to enjoy the stories I tell in these articles—a sort of repayment of or coming full circle from the stories he told me. But most of them, along with my three previous books about baseball, were written after his death. Two of the stories here, however, are about the relationship we forged through baseball, one about a meaningful road trip we took to Cooperstown the year before he died, the other about lessons his old glove taught me after his death. These stories about baseball, they outlive those in them and even those who tell them. I find something beautiful about that.

Chapter 1

IMMORTAL MOMENTS

THE RECONCILIATION OF
JUAN MARICHAL AND JOHN ROSEBORO

Two old rivals rewrote their final chapter, transforming the rage and violence of their past into an eternal friendship.

108 MAGAZINE, SUMMER 2007

Introduction

Like you, I'd seen the photograph. Juan Marichal bringing his bat down on the head of John Roseboro. But I didn't know much more than that. When I heard that Marichal had spoken at Roseboro's funeral, I wanted to know how that came about. I set out to find out what happened on August 22, 1965—and before, that had triggered their famous brawl—and what led to their very unlikely friendship.

Juan Marichal had dreaded the phone call. Barbara Fouch-Roseboro told him her husband Johnny, the former Dodgers catcher, had died. She asked Marichal to deliver a eulogy and to be an honorary pallbearer. Johnny would have wanted it. Marichal caught the first flight he could from the Dominican Republic to Los Angeles.

It was a sad journey for the former San Francisco Giants pitcher, yet it was also a closing of the circle. The two men, joined forever in the public mind by a single moment of violence 37 years earlier, had been eternally bound by that act.

The bonding took place slowly, rescuing one man's glory and erasing the other's guilt. And it did so out of public view, far from the old Dodgers-Giants rivalry that exploded that August afternoon in 1965 before 42,087 fans in San Francisco's Candlestick Park.

The rivalry between the Dodgers and the Giants—the most intense in baseball history, perhaps in all sports—had lost little when it moved from New York to the West Coast in 1958.

"We hated each other," writes Orlando Cepeda, a former Giants first baseman and outfielder, in his autobiography *Baby Bull.*

"Those Dodger-Giant games weren't baseball," says Andy Pafko, a left fielder with the Brooklyn Dodgers in the early 1950s, in Roger Kahn's *The Boys of Summer.* "They were civil war."

The rivalry always intensified when the teams were battling for the National League lead. Games were typically punctuated by insults, threats, and knockdown pitches. When the two teams met in a four-game series in late summer 1965, the Giants trailed the Dodgers by only a half-game.

Juan Marichal came to bat in the third inning on August 22, 1965, expecting to hit the dirt. That's where he had put leadoff man Maury Wills and cleanup hitter Ron Fairly after they had combined for Los Angeles' first run. Baseball's code called for retaliation—a high, inside fastball that screamed: "You can't get away with throwing at our guys."

On the mound stood the hardest thrower in baseball, Sandy Koufax. In the second inning, Koufax had fired a fastball over Willie Mays's head— more wild pitch than intentional warning. Koufax normally didn't throw at batters, but Marichal wondered if, under the circumstances, the Dodgers' ace might go after him.

Johnny Roseboro doubted it. He'd called for Koufax to knock down Mays, but Koufax had sailed the ball to the backstop. Roseboro believed that Koufax was "constitutionally incapable" of throwing at batters—too nice and too afraid of hurting them. Roseboro called for another inside pitch. He would set Marichal straight by himself. The stage was set for a scene of horrible violence never before witnessed on a major-league field.

*   *   *

Juan Marichal was an intimidating pitcher. In his signature windup, the right-hander reared back, kicked his left leg high—spikes nearly scraping the sky—dipped the knuckles of his right hand low to the dirt, and fired from his arsenal of pitches: curve, slider, screwball, and lightning fastball. The Dominican Dandy made his debut for the Giants in 1960 by one-hitting the Phillies, striking out 12. In 1963, his 25 wins—one of them a no-hitter—topped the National League. A workhorse who led the league in innings pitched in 1963 and in complete games in 1964, he threw a 16-inning shutout against the Braves in July 1963. By late August of 1965 he had posted a 19–9 record and had been selected as the MVP of that summer's All-Star Game.

The Dominican Republic native laughed readily. He was a prankster who hid teammates' car keys or startled them with firecrackers set off behind their backs. At the same time, he remained hypersensitive to any hint of mistreatment that violated his sense of justice. Marichal, 5-foot-11 and 185 pounds, could use his fists when necessary, like the New Year's Eve in a Santo Domingo nightclub when a mob swarmed him and he punched his way out of the club.

Marichal was born October 20, 1937, in a palm-bark shack in Laguna Verde, a poor village near the Dominican-Haitian border. As a young boy, only three years old, he lost his father—rum destroyed the man's liver. When Juan showed talent on the ball field, Ramfis Trujillo, son of dictator Rafael Trujillo, pressed the 17-year-old pitcher into service on the national team. Four years later, the Giants lured Marichal away, but Juan's family—his mother, brother, sister, 16 cousins, and nine nieces and nephews—remained in the Dominican Republic.

During the summer of 1965, he worried about them, as civil war shredded his homeland. In late April, shortly after the baseball season had started, President Lyndon Johnson sent 20,000 U.S. Marines to the Dominican Republic to quash a revolt that he believed would transform the Dominican into "a second Cuba." Throughout the summer, the conflict between the two heavily armed sides raged in the streets. The crossfire cut down countless innocent civilians.

The war weighed heavily on Marichal. Lying awake at night, kicking around his San Francisco home, driving to the ballpark, he wrestled with his worries. What if the bullets struck down someone he loved? The family home had no telephone, so he had to rely on slow-traveling international mail for word of his loved ones' safety—knowing the reports could be outdated by the time they arrived. He tried to shove away those worries when he took the mound, but the anxiety gnawed at him. "I really don't think Juan should have been playing at all," Willie Mays, his friend and teammate, told the *New York Times*. "He was pretty strung out, full of fear and anger, and holding it inside."

* * *

Johnny Roseboro had proven a solid replacement for Roy Campanella as the Dodgers' backstop since 1958. He had played in three All-Star Games and won a Gold Glove. Teammates had playfully nicknamed the laconic Roseboro "Gabby." Under his tough, quiet exterior beat a tender heart with a well-developed sense of justice, ready to right a wrong as necessary.

An African American born May 13, 1933, in Ashland, Ohio, Roseboro had moved to Los Angeles, where he bought a house. Driving home on the freeway from Dodger Stadium, Roseboro passed through the heart of the Watts ghetto. He saw fellow African Americans living in squalor unable to find work. Inadequate schools sentenced their children to more of the same. Frustration ignited and exploded in the infamous Watts riots on August 11, 1965, which raged for six days. The violence resulted in nearly three dozen fatalities and more than 1,000 injured. President Johnson dispatched the armored division of the National Guard, which occupied the burned-out war zone of Watts. Martial law was declared in south-central Los Angeles.

The racial violence so close to home pierced Roseboro. He watched the city burn, heard the toll of brothers and sisters killed. Even when he pulled on his uniform, scenes continued to play in his mind. He was distraught and distracted on the field. One night during those terrible six days, when he heard protestors planned to march down his street, he sat by the front door with a gun, "prepared to protect my property."

* * *

Mere days after the Watts riots ended, the Dodgers opened a critical four-game series in San Francisco. Only a game and a half separated the four contenders: the Dodgers, the Giants, the Milwaukee Braves, and the Cincinnati Reds.

Before the first game on August 19, Marichal spotted Roseboro in the right-field bullpen as the Giants finished batting practice and the Dodgers came onto the field. The two had a brief collegial conversation before the Dodgers won in 15 innings to increase their pennant lead to a game and a half.

The next night, a little-known incident took place that marked the first skirmish between Marichal and Roseboro.

Maury Wills led off the fifth for the Dodgers with a trick play, faking a bunt, luring Giants catcher Tom Haller out of his crouch, then tipping Haller's mitt as he pulled his bat back. Over howls of protest from the Giants, Wills was awarded first base for catcher's interference.

In the bottom of the inning, Giants leadoff hitter Matty Alou tried the same thing. The umpire ruled that Alou had not ticked Roseboro's mitt. The pitch, however, struck Roseboro hard in the chest protector. "Weasel bastard," he snarled. "If somebody hurts me, I'm gonna get one of you guys."

Marichal, Alou's best friend, responded to Roseboro. "Why do you get mad?" he shouted from the bench. "Haller doesn't get mad!"

Roseboro glared at the Giants dugout. "You sonofabitch, if you have something to say, come out and say it to my face."

Marichal, standing next to the Giants' manager, didn't move off the dugout steps.

"If he doesn't shut his big mouth, he'll get a ball right behind his ear," Roseboro told Alou, who relayed the message to Marichal.

After the game, won by the Giants, Roseboro happened to run into Cepeda in the parking lot.

"I told him to tell Marichal that if he had the guts to tangle with me, fine, but if not, to quit wolfin' at me from behind the manager's back," Roseboro writes in his 1978 autobiography *Glory Days with the Dodgers.*

After watching the Dodgers defeat the Giants in 11 innings on Saturday, the hometown fans came to Candlestick Park on Sunday afternoon expecting victory. The starting pitcher would be their ace, Marichal, who had defeated the Dodgers 10 straight times at home. But in the bottom of the third inning, the Dodgers led 2–1, as Marichal led off the Giants' half of the inning.

Koufax's first pitch curved across the plate for a strike. Marichal was ready to swing at the second pitch, but Koufax's fastball came in low and inside.

Roseboro dropped the ball, moved inside to pick it up, and whizzed a throw past Marichal's face. Marichal later said the ball clipped his ear. He turned to face Roseboro. "Why did you do that?" he demanded.

The 5-foot-11, 195-pound Roseboro stepped toward Marichal, ready to punch him. "Fuck you!"

Marichal saw the catcher in his mask and chest protector advancing on him. He backed up, remembering Roseboro's threats, repeated by Alou and Cepeda. Fear took over.

Marichal raised his bat over his helmet and brought it down on Roseboro's head like he was splitting firewood. The blow did not strike squarely but did open a two-inch gash above Roseboro's left eye.

Roseboro lunged and flailed at Marichal. Marichal chopped at Roseboro with his bat. Plate umpire Shag Crawford attempted to intervene.

Koufax rushed from the mound. Charlie Fox, the Giants' third-base coach, ran in to separate the combatants. Tito Fuentes raced from the on-deck circle, bat in hand. The benches emptied. Reinforcements dashed in from the bullpens. The brawl raged on the field for 14 minutes.

Marichal retreated to the dugout, still brandishing his bat. "I didn't want them to take the bat away from me," he said. "I know if they take the bat away then everybody will hit me."

Roseboro chased him, but Mays—Marichal's teammate and Roseboro's friend—intercepted him. "John, stop it, stop fighting," Mays pleaded. He tenderly wiped Roseboro's head and led him off the field, his Giants uniform splattered with his friend's blood.

*   *   *

The Candlestick fans booed Roseboro. He flashed them the finger.

Roseboro wanted to stay in the game, but Dodgers manager Walt Alston insisted he have his wound stitched. Roseboro had to walk across the outfield to the clubhouse entrance. The fans taunted him. He bent over and patted his rear—conveying an unmistakable nonverbal message. San Francisco police, concerned for Roseboro's safety and worried about further violence, escorted him to a taxi stand, where he caught a cab directly to the airport.

Crawford ejected Marichal, who listened to the rest of the game on the radio in the clubhouse. Play resumed with police patrolling the dugouts and playing field. Later in the same inning, Mays stroked a three-run homer 450 feet, and the Giants went on to win 4–3. The series finished the way it had started: the Giants a half-game behind the Dodgers.

*   *   *

In the days immediately afterward, anger ruled Roseboro. When reporters asked him what sort of penalty he felt Marichal deserved, he said, "He and I in a room together for about ten minutes." Within two weeks of the incident, he sued Marichal for $110,000 in actual and punitive damages.

For his part, Marichal regretted that he had injured Roseboro with his bat, yet he felt misunderstood and unfairly vilified. "First of all, I want to apologize for using the bat," he said the next day. "I am sorry for what I did, but I was afraid of him."

*   *   *

Never before had any ballplayer clubbed another player during a game. Fellow players, fans, and sportswriters condemned Marichal's action, calling it "outrageous," "disgraceful," and "cowardly." Howard Cosell referred to it as "dastardly." Some thought Marichal should serve time for assault; others called for his ban from baseball. "It has to be a pretty warped instinct for one ballplayer to flail another on the skull with a bat," Arthur Daley wrote in the *New York Times*.

National League president Warren Giles fined Marichal $1,750 and suspended him for eight playing dates. He also prohibited him from pitching in Los Angeles in early September when the Giants next played the Dodgers. In a telegram to Marichal, Giles chastised his "repugnant actions" and wrote, "My investigation indicated there were underlying currents by others throughout the series, but your sudden and violent action was unprovoked and obnoxious and must be penalized."

The fine was the largest levied against a player up to that time, and the suspension was one of the longest. Marichal would miss at least two starts, but some judged the punishment softer than the crime. "That's sickening," Ron Fairly said. "It should be a suspension of 1,750 days."

By calling Marichal's action "unprovoked," Giles exonerated Roseboro from any wrongdoing, in spite of his throw past Marichal's face.

Giles's actions rallied Marichal supporters, especially in the Bay Area. California secretary of state Frank Jordan offered to start a fundraising campaign to pay Marichal's fine. "Why, they didn't even throw Roseboro out!" he wrote in a letter to the *San Francisco Examiner*. "He gets off pretty damn clean."

"That was a lethal weapon Roseboro used, throwing the ball that distance by Marichal's head," said Lon Simmons, the Giants' broadcaster who called the game on KSFO radio. "It was wrong for Marichal to hit him with the bat, but tell me, what are you going to do if you've got a bat in your hands? He had a means of defense and he used it."

Marichal's suspension stood—making neither the Giants nor the Dodgers happy. The Giants, however, ended the season two games behind the first-place Dodgers, and sportswriters speculated that Marichal's suspension and two missed starts had cost his team the pennant.

The incident dogged Marichal during the winter. Everywhere he went, all people wanted to talk about was his fight with Roseboro.

The next spring, Marichal faced Roseboro in an exhibition game. Almost 8,000 people crammed into the Phoenix ballpark on April 3, 1966, and another 1,000 stood on a hill beyond the left-field fence. Somebody had suggested the two shake hands before the game at home plate. Neither initiated the gesture. "If he says hello to me, I'll say hello to him," Roseboro said. "But I won't pose for pictures. Nobody would be asking us to pose for pictures if it wasn't for the fight."

Roseboro came to bat in the top of the second with two on and one out. The crowd cheered lustily. "Nobody really knew what to expect," Harry Jupiter wrote for *Sport* magazine. "It was like the crowd that packs the Indianapolis Speedway every Memorial Day. Nobody wants to see anybody get hurt or killed, but if it's going to happen . . ."

Marichal's first pitch was outside. Roseboro worked the count to 2–2 then hit a slider cleanly to right field. The ball hopped high over the charging right fielder's head, and Roseboro rounded the bases with a fluke inside-the-park home run. Roseboro flied out in his next at-bat against Marichal. Any fans who had come to witness the conclusion of lingering business between Marichal and Roseboro left unsatisfied.

The two faced each other many times over the next two years, before Roseboro finished out his career in the American League with the Twins and Senators, retiring in 1970. Marichal never threw at him. The lawsuit was finally settled in 1972, when Marichal agreed to pay Roseboro $7,000.

* * *

Once his initial anger waned, Roseboro felt remorse over his part in the fight. He knew people remembered him best for "the fight"—not his six All-Star Game selections, two Gold Gloves, nor the two Koufax no-hitters he caught. People would always talk about August 1965 when they approached him in restaurants, on business phone calls, even when he lay dying in the hospital. That wasn't how he wanted to be remembered. He admitted in his autobiography—and continued to confess until his death in 2002—that he had provoked the incident.

The scorn Marichal endured moved Roseboro to compassion. "There's no question that the bit hurt him more than it hurt me," Roseboro reflects in his memoir. "It soiled him. It has stuck to him like a stain. I think some people think of him hitting me with the bat more than they think of him as the great pitcher he was."

And a great pitcher he was, the dominant pitcher of the 1960s. Marichal won more than 20 games six years out of seven, including three seasons of 25 or more wins. His 191 victories during the decade topped Bob Gibson's 164 victories, Don Drysdale's 158, and Koufax's 137. Still, the boos continued. He received nasty letters and violent threats. He said they didn't bother him, but he stashed the letters in a closet and eventually admitted to the *Saturday Evening Post*, "They [boos] hurt. Trouble with baseball is that always they [fans] want more, more, more . . . without thinking of what suffering they bring a player who happens to be down."

Matty Alou's brother Jesus, Marichal's countryman and roommate on the road, explained why the derision cut so deep. "Juan needs love," Alou said. "You see, we Dominicans do not play just for money, but for appreciation."

* * *

Roseboro and Marichal did not discuss their fight for more than 10 years. Finally, at an old-timer's game that brought them together in the mid-1970s, they shook hands. Roseboro joked that maybe they shouldn't because once they did, the sportswriters wouldn't have anything to write about.

Previously, Roseboro had made a magnanimous gesture, when a fading Marichal joined the Dodgers before the 1975 season. Dodgers fans objected and refused to let go of the resentment. Roseboro, however, publicly urged the fans to welcome him to the team.

Knowing Marichal was only a shadow of his dominant self, Roseboro even offered the aging right-hander some friendly advice, telling him he had to keep hitters off the plate by throwing inside. "He just smiled," Roseboro wrote. "I guess he couldn't do it anymore."

In just two games with the Dodgers, Marichal gave up nine runs and struck out only one batter in six innings. "If I can't pitch as well as I want to, I can't take your money," he told Dodgers owner Walter O'Malley and retired.

When he became eligible for induction into the National Baseball Hall of Fame in 1981, Marichal had the numbers to justify immediate selection: a 243–142 record over 16 seasons, 2.89 ERA, and 2,303 strikeouts. Still, members of the Baseball Writers' Association of America failed to grant him the necessary votes. The next year, he again fell short. In the same way that the fight had overshadowed his success during his playing career, it threatened to permanently scar his legacy.

Marichal feared that he would not be remembered for his one-hit rookie debut, nor for his 16-inning shutout, nor for his nine All-Star Games. Just for an ugly August afternoon in 1965, when concern for loved ones threatened by a civil war, the tension of a pennant race, and fear for his own safety spilled out in a violent and regrettable action. He phoned Roseboro.

"John," he said, "the sportswriters won't let me in the Hall of Fame because I did something terrible."

"You didn't do anything terrible," Roseboro replied. "It was a game."

"Neither of them considered each other enemies," recalls Barbara Fouch-Roseboro. "They said it was just a game and the sportswriters had made too much of it."

Roseboro saw how Marichal had suffered from the bad press. That bothered him. The guilt he felt for his part had never completely left him. He was ready to forgive and forget. Why couldn't everyone else feel the same? Roseboro wanted to clear Marichal's name in a public way.

He accepted Marichal's invitation to attend a charity golf tournament in the Dominican Republic that the former Giants pitcher hosted. Marichal provided Roseboro, Barbara, and her daughter Morgan with comfortable accommodations. Morgan hit it off with Juan's three daughters, while Barbara and Alma Rosa, Juan's wife, also enjoyed one another's company. It was the beginning of a beautiful friendship.

Roseboro and Barbara, who had formed a public relations company that became one of the leading firms in Los Angeles, also supported Marichal's inclusion into the Hall of Fame. In his third year of eligibility, he was elected with 84 percent of the vote. In his 1983 induction speech, Marichal thanked Roseboro.

"It was the most wonderful thing to see them become that close to each other," Fouch-Roseboro says. "That went on until the day of John's death."

The two men saw themselves in one another. They discovered in each other a quiet, gracious man who had been a fierce competitor.

"In many ways, Juan and John were alike in their makeups," observed Fred Claire, an executive with the Dodgers from 1969 to 1998. "I'm sure that was part of the bond between them."

In 1991, the Dodgers sent Roseboro to the Dominican Republic to manage the Licey Tigers. He led them to the Caribbean Championship. Marichal drove to the ballpark to see him. They chatted about baseball and life in the Dominican Republic. When Roseboro's family visited, Marichal provided a condominium as their home away from home. The golf tournament had sparked a family friendship that continues today. "We see each other, send pictures, call one another," Fouch-Roseboro says. "Juan calls to see how I'm doing."

Roseboro's heart had started to deteriorate in the late 1980s. When Marichal discovered how serious Roseboro's condition had become in 2002, he offered his prayers. When Roseboro died on August 16, 2002, at the age of 69, Marichal boarded a plane headed north.

In his eulogy eight days later, Marichal spoke respectfully of the man with whom he had once fought and later befriended. He moved the audience at the Forest Lawn Mortuary to laughter and tears. He told Barbara and the Roseboro family that he regretted his fight with John but treasured the gift of forgiveness that Roseboro had left him. "I wish I could have had John Roseboro as my catcher."

Postscript

I was so taken by Marichal and Roseboro's story that I continued to research it after writing this article and found enough material to write a book that provided deeper context for their fight and the friendship that later developed. *The Fight of Their Lives: How Juan Marichal and John Roseboro Turned Baseball's Ugliest Brawl into a Story of Forgiveness and Redemption* was published in 2014.

ON THE WAY TO 714

Hank Aaron had to navigate racial prejudice and a media circus on his way to the milestone represented by baseball's most iconic number.

MEMORIES & DREAMS, SPRING 2020

Introduction

I turned nine the summer of 1973 when Hank Aaron pursued Babe Ruth's career home run record, old enough to be swept up in the drama of the moment, but still innocent to the ugly racism that served as its subtext. I remember watching the historic game on April 8, 1974, on the Zenith television in our family room; I later hung a poster of the moment on my bedroom wall—the ball circled in its flight toward Aaron's immortality. It wasn't until I came of age that I learned the full story.

For nearly 40 years, 714 was the measure of a hitter's greatness. More so than 60 or 61 or .406. Those were seasonal marks. Even 4,191, Ty Cobb's career hit total (later amended to 4,189 but not broken until 1985), deferred to 714. Not only was it easier to remember, 714 marked the number of times one man had thrilled fans with his power in ways no other mortal seemed capable of.

The number 714, of course, was synonymous with Babe Ruth. For baseball fans, no explanation is required; 714 was woven into his legend, same as "the curse of the Bambino," his generosity with children having been a young orphan himself, even his appetite for hot dogs.

When Ruth retired in 1935 at 714, no one else had hit more than 378 (Lou Gehrig). Indeed, he had eclipsed the record of 136 in 1921 and reigned as the Home Run King while he played. For 14 years, every home run he hit provided another jewel in his crown. It would be five years after Ruth retired before anyone even reached 500 (Jimmie Foxx), and by 1970, only four other major-league hitters had slugged 500 career taters (Mel Ott, Ted Williams, Mickey Mantle, and Hank Aaron). Even as Willie Mays and Aaron reached 600, they still remained far behind Ruth's total—714 had achieved iconic status that seemed untouchable. No other number in baseball inspired the reverence it did.

People forget Ruth had a .342 lifetime batting average over 22 seasons. And that he had 2,214 career RBIs. After Roger Maris broke his single-season home run record of 60 (knocking out 61 in 1961), 714 stood alone as the number that defined Ruth's greatness. And well it should. He hit the bulk of those (688) from 1919 to 1934, which means he averaged 43 home runs a season for 16 straight years. No other player had demonstrated such consistent mastery of the long ball. And, it was thought, no other player ever would.

Until the unthinkable unfolded. During the summer of 1973, Aaron put himself within reach of 714, the mark many thought would stand forever. He began the season at 673 and steadily edged closer and closer, making the impossible seem possible. If anyone could break Ruth's record, it seemed Aaron could. Though he famously never hit more than 47 home runs in one season, Aaron matched Ruth's consistency, averaging 37 home runs per season over 19 years, from 1955 through 1973.

By the time he knocked out No. 700 on July 21, 1973, and joined Ruth in the rarified air only they inhaled as the greatest home run hitters of all time, Aaron had excited fans and electrified the nation. His pursuit created a media circus—such as it was in the days before the 24-hour news cycle, MLB.com, and social media. Reporters from national magazines besieged him at the ballpark. An NBC-TV camera crew shadowed him for weeks. When he went fishing in Mobile, Alabama, on a day off, three boats full of reporters and photographers stalked him.

Letters poured in from all over the country, by the hundreds daily. The overwhelming majority were positive, from fans cheering him on. They recognized him as a great player making history and wanted to be witness to it. But some of the letters, about one in nine, were littered with racial slurs and death threats. The number 714 wasn't a benign number. It represented the legend of a beloved white man now threatened by a Black man. And that exposed the underbelly of America's bigotry.

"It was just amazing that the myth of Ruth and this home run number was a kind of white supremacy symbol for many people," Reverend Jesse Jackson observed.

When Aaron went public about the hate mail, he received an outpouring of support from other players and fans, but it did not stop the taunts from the stands or the steady flow of nasty letters. Nor did it squelch the threats to Aaron and his family. He traveled with two plainclothes policemen as bodyguards, checked into hotels under an alias on the road, and feared for his children's safety.

The prejudice seemed to reach baseball's highest ranks. It had been only 26 years since Jackie Robinson had crossed Major League Baseball's color line. While the establishment had reluctantly opened its doors to Black players, it did not seem ready to write them into the record books. When Aaron joined Ruth in the two-man 700 club, Commissioner Bowie Kuhn was conspicuously absent from the stands and neglected to send a telegram of congratulations.

Though Aaron was a private and reticent man who did not court controversy, he felt compelled to call out Kuhn. "I believed he would have shown more interest in the record if a white player were involved," he explains in his autobiography *I Had a Hammer*. "And I also believed it was my duty to call attention to discrimination in baseball."

Aaron made his strongest statements with the bat. Every home run he hit chipped away at the notion of white supremacy. And advanced the cause of a Black American hero.

But after Aaron reached 700 in late July, his pace slowed. Under the glare of the national media scrutiny and the daily onslaught of hate mail, he hit only one more dinger in July and five in August. He entered the final month of the 1973 season sitting at 706, eight shy of Ruth's milestone. It became a race against time, lengthening shadows, deeper bullpens, and seasonal fatigue for the 39-year-old Aaron. He knew he didn't have to reach 714 that season, but he wanted to so he could relieve himself of the pressure.

When he hit No. 712 on September 22 with five games left to play, the record seemed within reach, maybe. All that month the *New York Times* ran a front-page count of Aaron's progress. NBC interrupted scheduled programming to show his latest home run. By the last week of the season, fans tuned into the heightened drama tensed with anticipation.

But then a week went by before he knocked out No. 713. And, when he hit three singles but no home runs in the Braves' final game, that's where he stayed, stalled for a long winter at 713. It seemed an eternity until he would get another at-bat.

Once he finally did—six months later on Opening Day of the 1974 season—Aaron promptly satisfied the fans he had tantalized and left suspended with No. 714. Four days later at Atlanta Stadium, Aaron faced Al Downing of the Los Angeles Dodgers in a fourth-inning moment seared into the memories of fans of a certain age—and preserved for younger ones on YouTube. On April 8, 1974, when Aaron put Downing's second pitch over the left-field fence, trotted around the bases with a brief escort from two young men, and hugged his mother at home plate, he stepped in front of Babe Ruth and was hailed as the new Home Run King. "What a marvelous moment for baseball," Vin Scully said on the national broadcast. "What a marvelous moment for the country and the world. A Black man is getting a standing ovation in the Deep South for breaking the record of an all-time baseball idol."

Forty-six years have passed since that night in Atlanta. Aaron hit 40 more home runs to retire with 755. Barry Bonds reached 714 in 2006, passed Aaron a year later, and retired with 762 career home runs. For his achievement and the quiet dignity with which he accomplished it, Aaron has earned an exhibit all his own in the National Baseball Hall of Fame. As for Bonds, though his record is tainted by suspicion of steroid assistance, he may one day be enshrined himself.

Yet it is unlikely 755 or 762—or some higher number in the future— will ever achieve the legendary stature their forebear the Babe did with his 714.

Postscript

Parts of this article are drawn from a book I wrote about the 1973 baseball season, *Hammerin' Hank, George Almighty and the Say Hey Kid: The Year That Changed Baseball Forever* (2008), in which Aaron's pursuit of Ruth's iconic record became one of several story lines. The others follow George Steinbrenner infusing big money into the game with his purchase of the New York Yankees; Willie Mays passing the torch to Reggie Jackson, who redefined what it meant to be a superstar; and Orlando Cepeda extending his career in the first season of the designated hitter.

HARVEY HADDIX'S HEARTBREAK

The Pirates' pitcher suffered the worst tough-luck loss ever.

MLB INSIDERS CLUB MAGAZINE, JUNE 2009

Introduction

In the song "Harvey Haddix" on its 2008 album *Frozen Ropes and Dying Quails*, the Baseball Project sings, "We're drawn to tragic stories, the ones that suit us best." Like those boys in the band (whom I got to see perform at the 2015 SABR Conference), I was certainly drawn to the story of Haddix's heart-wrenching loss, which became all the more incredible the more I learned about it.

Harvey Haddix started thinking about it in the fourth inning—he hadn't given up a hit. True to baseball superstition, his Pittsburgh teammates didn't say anything to him, but Pirates radio announcer Bob Prince told fans tuned into KDKA-AM, "First nine men up and down." On a warm and muggy Tuesday evening at Milwaukee's County Stadium, Haddix—who was 20–9 as a rookie in 1953, would win two games in the 1960 World Series and 136 games in his 14-year major-league career—was pitching the game of his life. The 33-year-old southpaw's performance on May 26, 1959, would immortalize him as the game's greatest loser.

That evening, the diminutive Haddix—who stood 5-foot-9, weighed 155 pounds wet, and had earned his nickname "The Kitten" pitching for the St. Louis Cardinals in the shadow of Harry "The Cat" Brecheen—dominated the two-time defending National League champion Braves' heavy-hitting lineup. His fastball jumped and hit its spots; his hard slider grooved and nicked the corners. The humid night let him grip the ball a bit better, which made his pitches break sharper. The Kitten purred.

Milwaukee's Johnny Logan, always tough on the Pirates, came the closest to getting a hit. In the third inning, he rapped a sharp line drive in the hole between third and short within the range of regular Pirates shortstop Dick Groat. But Groat was on the bench, taking a game off. His replacement, Dick Schofield, speared Logan's drive. Three innings later, Logan hit a grounder to short that took a bad hop and looked like it would skip through for a base hit, but Schofield came up with the ball and threw out Logan.

The players could tell by glancing at the zero on the scoreboard under "hits" that Haddix had the no-hitter going, but by about the fifth, someone on the Pirates' bench whispered, "He hasn't had anybody on base yet." By the ninth, they were whispering, "Son of a gun, he's got a perfect game, we've got to win it here."

Problem was, even though Haddix and his teammates managed 12 hits off Braves starter Lew Burdette, they couldn't push a run across the plate. In the seventh, Pirates left fielder Bob Skinner hit a drive to right field that would have easily cleared the fence had the wind not come up a couple of innings earlier. The stiff breeze held up Skinner's drive, and Braves right fielder Hank Aaron caught the ball against the fence. "If the wind hadn't been blowing in, that would've been a home run, and we would've won the ball game in nine innings," Pirates pitcher Elroy Face says.

With soft rains falling occasionally and lightning skipping across the night sky, the game marched on in a scoreless tie. Haddix continued to set down the Braves, one-two-three, inning after inning. Only seven pitchers to date had thrown perfect games. After Haddix had retired 24 consecutive batters, Prince told KDKA listeners, "Don't go away. We are on the verge of baseball history."

When Haddix took the hill in the bottom of the ninth, he wasn't sure about the perfect game—he thought he might've walked someone earlier. He had lost a no-hitter once before in the ninth inning, back in 1953, when the Phillies' Richie Ashburn had singled to right field off a Haddix curve. No doubt that played through Haddix's thoughts as he struck out Andy Pafko, retired Logan on a fly ball to left, and struck out Burdette. Up in the radio booth, Prince screamed in excitement, "Harvey Haddix has pitched a perfect no-hit, no-run game!"

But the scoreless tie sent the game into extra innings. Haddix, who had singled in the third inning but been stranded at third base, came to bat in the top of the 10th with two outs and a runner on first. Braves catcher Del Crandall said, "Say, you're pitching a pretty good game." Haddix grounded out to the pitcher.

But he was perfect again on the mound. The Braves were stealing Pirates catcher Smoky Burgess's signs—they could see his fingers below his crouch—and relaying them to the Braves' batters, but even when they knew what was coming, Haddix was throwing so well they couldn't touch him. He retired Del Rice, Eddie Mathews, and Aaron in order.

When his Pirates teammates failed to score in their half of the 11th—ending the inning by hitting into their third double play of the game—Haddix had to do it again. By now, his arm was tiring. The seven men who had thrown perfect games had been done after nine innings. (In the 10 perfect games since, none lasted more than nine innings. Four others have thrown unofficial perfect games in fewer than nine innings.) Wes Covington smashed a long drive to center—the hardest ball hit off Haddix so far that night—but Pirates center fielder Bill Virdon snagged it at the fence for the second out. The next batter, Crandall, hit a towering drive deep to center, but once again Virdon was there to preserve Haddix's perfect game.

Haddix was perfect again in the 12th, though he gave up another fly ball to center field. The Pirates failed to score in the top of the 13th. They had put runners on base in each of the extra innings, badly wanting to win it for Haddix, but couldn't bring them home. In the 12th and 13th, Pirates batters singled with two out, only to die on base. The Pirates stranded eight runners that night. "We had some chances but just couldn't get the base hit when we needed it," Schofield says.

Feeling lucky in the 13th, Braves first baseman Joe Adcock told the first-base ump that the Braves would win it in their half of the inning. Felix Mantilla led off for the Braves. Haddix thought he had caught Mantilla looking for his ninth strikeout of the game, but the ump called the pitch a ball. Mantilla hit Haddix's next pitch to third. Pirates third baseman Don Hoak fielded the ball, but his throw bounced at the first baseman's feet and got by him. The Pirates argued that they had tagged Mantilla out as he rounded first but to no avail. The error spoiled Haddix's perfect game, but he still had the longest no-hitter on record going.

Mathews's sacrifice bunt moved Mantilla to second. Haddix intentionally walked Aaron to face Adcock. Haddix's first pitch missed. Not wanting to throw a curve like the one Ashburn had hit in 1953, Haddix went with his slider. He wanted to throw it down and away, but the ball stayed up, and Adcock, who would hit 25 home runs that season, clobbered it to right-center field. Adcock paused for a moment but then began rounding the bases as the ball cleared the fence to the right of the 390-foot sign.

The Milwaukee players spilled onto the field, and Aaron joined the jubilant celebration after touching second. The ump called Adcock out for passing Aaron on the basepath. The next day, National League president Warren Giles would rule Adcock's hit a double, reducing the final game score to 1–0. But no matter how many runs the Braves scored, what counted was that Haddix had retired 36 consecutive batters, struck out eight—and lost.

Afterward in the clubhouse, he asked reporters for some time alone. When he finally spoke to them, he was gracious, acknowledging the fielding help of his teammates—naming Schofield and Virdon—but the disappointment showed on his face. He took a call from Burdette, who cracked, "You've got to scatter your hits better," then added sincerely, "You pitched the greatest game that's ever been pitched in the history of baseball." High praise, but small consolation in the moment.

Haddix showered, dressed, and walked to an all-night diner with his roommate and fellow pitcher Bob Friend. They ate bacon and eggs but didn't talk much. "That was one hell of a game," Friend finally said. "Do you know what you did?"

"Yeah, I know," Haddix replied. "But we were on the wrong end."

In the years afterward, that game—the near-perfect, 13-inning loss—always came up: at old-timer's games, reunions with teammates, banquets. Seemed wherever Haddix went, the specter of that game followed. It had defined him and in no small part by the way he always talked about it graciously.

Three years before Haddix died in 1994, he suffered an additional loss. An MLB committee on statistical accuracy changed the definition of a no-hitter to a game that ends after nine or more innings with one team failing to get a hit. That wiped 50 no-hitters from the record books, including Haddix's 12-inning gem. "That was ridiculous," Schofield says. "If that's not a no-hitter, there's no such animal."

Still, 50 years later, many baseball purists consider Haddix's performance—no-hitter or not, loss and all—the greatest pitching display ever. "I don't think enough credit has been given to Harvey for that game," Aaron says. "Had it been pitched in New York, it would have been different, but I don't know of anybody who has pitched a better game."

Postscript

Since this article was published in 2009, six more men have pitched perfect games in the majors: Mark Buehrle, Dallas Braden, Roy Halladay, Philip Humber, Matt Cain, and Felix Hernandez. Seven if you count Armando Galarraga. Harvey Haddix gained a heartbreak companion in the Detroit Tigers' right-hander who pitched a perfect game on June 2, 2010, at Comerica Park. Twenty-seven up, 27 down—except Jim Joyce, the first-base ump, saw the last one wrong, calling the runner safe though he clearly had not beaten the throw. Galarraga promptly retired the next batter to complete what became known as the "28-out perfect game." Afterward, upon realizing his error, Joyce sought out Galarraga and tearfully apologized. Galarraga graciously forgave Joyce and gave him a hug.

Chapter 2

BASEBALL DURING WARTIME

TERROR IN THE TRENCHES

Ty Cobb, Christy Mathewson, and Branch Rickey joined the Gas & Flame Division during the Great War—but only two made it out safely.

MEMORIES & DREAMS, SPRING 2017

Introduction

Much has been written about baseball players like Bob Feller, Ted Williams, Hank Greenberg, and the rest answering the call during World War II, less about those who served in the First World War. So I was intrigued when I heard about how the paths of several future Hall of Famers converged in the Gas & Flame Division—and its consequences.

The Great War initiated chemical warfare on a grand scale. It began with tear gas in the summer of 1914, and by 1917, the German, French, and British were assailing one another with deadly chlorine, phosgene, and mustard gas.

The United States responded by creating the Chemical Warfare Service in the summer of 1918 to combat the gas attacks. The elite corps, commonly called the "Gas & Flame Division," recruited top athletes to fill its ranks. "We do not just want good young athletes," Major General William L. Sibert said. "We are searching for good strong men, endowed with extraordinary capabilities to lead others during gas attacks."

During the course of the war, 227 major leaguers served the United States through various branches of the armed forces. Several Hall of Famers, including Christy Mathewson, Branch Rickey, George Sisler, and Ty Cobb, answered the specific call issued by the Chemical Warfare Service. At least one may have paid the ultimate price as a result.

* * *

As the war intensified overseas, Major League Baseball owners, complying with the wishes of the federal government, reduced the 1918 season from 154 games to 128. But they resisted the draft, arguing that baseball should be considered an "essential industry," one that buoyed the spirit of democracy, so their players would be exempt from conscription. Secretary of War Newton D. Baker did not agree. On July 20, he decreed that "players in the draft age must obtain employment calculated to aid in the successful prosecution of the war or shoulder guns and fight."

As a result, many players sought employment in defense industries stateside, where they were able to continue playing ball safely on company teams. The 38-year-old Mathewson, whose 373 career pitching victories and 2.13 ERA over 17 seasons would make him a member of the National Baseball Hall of Fame's 1936 class, was too old to be drafted but still felt compelled to join the cause on the front lines. In late August 1918, the skipper of the Cincinnati Reds resigned his post and became Captain Mathewson, shipping to France for training with the new Gas & Flame Division.

Percy Haughton, perhaps best remembered as Harvard's football coach, resigned as president of the Boston Braves in July to join the division as well, and convinced St. Louis Cardinals president Branch Rickey, then 36, to enlist. Rickey was commissioned as a major and put in charge of the division.

Rickey in turn recruited St. Louis Browns standout first baseman George Sisler, whom he had managed at the University of Michigan and with the Browns. Sisler, 25, looked up to Rickey as a mentor and was easily persuaded to join the elite corps. After finishing the 1918 season, Sisler was commissioned as a second lieutenant and assigned to Camp Humphries in Virginia.

Ty Cobb, the Detroit Tigers' 31-year-old hitting machine, had been granted a deferment since he had a wife and three children dependent upon him, but he refused to remain on the sidelines. "I feel mean every time I look at a casualty list," he said in July. "I feel I must give up baseball at the close of the season and do my duty by my country in the best way possible."

The following month, he signed up for the Gas & Flame Division, explaining, "Christy Mathewson and Branch Rickey are in Chemical—they are guys I like and are friends." Commissioned a captain, Cobb finished the season with the Tigers, collected his 10th American League batting title with a .382 average, and joined Mathewson, Rickey, and Haughton with the 28th Division at the Allied Expeditionary Forces Headquarters in Chaumont, France, 120 miles south of Paris, on November 2.

The men of the Gas & Flame Division were charged with advancing across no-man's land under cover of an artillery barrage, spraying liquid flames from tanks strapped to their backs, and tossing gas-filled bombs like grenades into enemy trenches. They were still undergoing training when Cobb arrived. He and his baseball mates served as instructors, conducting realistic readiness drills, one of which sent soldiers into airtight chambers where actual poisonous gas was released.

One day the drill didn't go right. Several men—including Cobb and Mathewson—missed the signal to snap on their masks. Suddenly they were inhaling poisonous gas, and the scene erupted into chaos. Cobb finally managed to get his mask on and groped his way to the door past a tangle of screaming men and thrashing bodies. "Trying to lead the men out was hopeless," he said. "It was each one for himself."

Eight of his comrades died that day, their lungs ravaged by the gas. Eight more were crippled for several days. Cobb felt "Divine Providence" had spared his life, but Mathewson wheezed and hacked up congestion. "Ty, I got a good dose of the stuff," he told Cobb. "I feel terrible."

*   *   *

Before the division engaged in actual combat with the enemy, armistice was declared on November 11, 1918. Rickey returned to the States in time to spend Christmas with his family. Since the fighting was over, the War Department gave Major League Baseball permission to return to its normal operations with a full season in 1919. Rickey resumed his role as president of the Cardinals, managed the team for seven seasons, and built it into a champion with his famed farm system. He was inducted into the Hall of Fame by the Veterans Committee in 1967.

Sisler, who had been preparing to deploy when the armistice was signed, was honorably discharged from the Gas & Flame Division and returned to the Browns, where he established himself as one of the game's greatest hitters. His 257 hits in 1920 stood as the most in a single season for 84 years. In 1922, he set a record for a consecutive-game hitting streak, reaching safely in 41 games, and finished the season with a .420 average. A lifetime .340 hitter, Sisler was inducted into the Hall of Fame in 1939.

Cobb came back to the United States on the first ship out of France, arriving in Hoboken, New Jersey, on December 17. Still coughing up fluid from the drill gone wrong and feeling lousy, he announced his retirement from baseball.

He changed his mind once he started to feel better and the 1919 season approached. Then 32, Cobb returned to the Tigers, won his 12th and final batting title with a .384 average, and played another 10 seasons before retiring for real in 1928 at age 41 with a .366 lifetime average, which remains the highest of all time. He joined Mathewson in the Hall of Fame's inaugural class.

Mathewson had written Reds owner Garry Herrmann that he would be returning in time to manage the 1919 campaign, but Herrmann had not received his letter and hired a replacement. So Mathewson accepted a position as assistant manager under John McGraw with the team he had starred for as a pitcher, the New York Giants. But a cough that had stricken him after the botched gas-mask drill continued to dog him. His fading health forced him to retire after the 1920 season.

Doctors examined him in 1921 and diagnosed him with tuberculosis. The disease had killed his brother in 1917, and it is possible that Mathewson had been exposed to it through him. It is also possible that the mustard gas he inhaled had weakened his respiratory system, making him more vulnerable to contracting the disease. At any rate, he was sent to the tuberculosis sanitarium in the Adirondacks mountain village of Saranac Lake, New York, where he was not expected to live more than six weeks.

Mathewson spent two years convalescing and felt strong enough to return to baseball in February 1923 when Emil Fuchs, the new owner of the Boston Braves, named him president of the team. His physicians cautioned Matthewson not to work himself too hard. But he did not know any other way. In the spring of 1925, he caught a cold he couldn't shake, and his cough returned. He went back to Saranac Lake to recuperate.

In September, it looked like Mathewson might be improving, but then he took a turn for the worse and on October 7, the first day of the 1925 World Series played between the Pittsburgh Pirates and Washington Senators, Mathewson died at the age of 45. The official cause of death was tuberculosis pneumonia.

The following day, before the second game of the World Series, players from the Pirates and Senators wore black armbands to honor Mathewson. The 44,000 fans at Forbes Field stood while the flag was lowered to half-mast and sang "Nearer My God to Thee."

Cobb attended Mathewson's funeral two days later in Lewiston, Pennsylvania. The Pennsylvania native was laid to rest in a cemetery next to his alma mater, Bucknell University, where Mathewson had starred for both the football and baseball teams. "[He] looked peaceful in that coffin," Cobb said. "That damned gas got him and nearly got me."

Postscript

In F. Scott Fitzgerald's novel *This Side of Paradise*, the main character, Amory Blaine, wonders "whether [Mordecai] Three-finger Brown was really a better pitcher than Mathewson." He wasn't. Mathewson outdid him in most every career category, most notably with a 99.8 WAR (wins above replacement) over 17 seasons to Brown's 57.2 over 14. Sorry, Amory.

EQUAL OPPORTUNITY

The GI World Series of 1945 featured unlikely heroes who would not have been heralded at home.

MEMORIES & DREAMS, FALL 2020

Introduction

After receiving an email from a reader of one of my books who mentioned Sam Nahem as an overlooked figure by baseball historians, I poked around a bit and discovered this story about his role in the World Series played by American troops in Europe during the denouement of World War II.

Sunday afternoon, September 2, 1945, resembled any other at the ballpark: sunshine splashed across green grass, fans drinking beer, live radio broadcast, the Stars and Stripes fluttering from the flagpole—except for the ballpark. This game was played at *Stadion der Hitlerjugend*, the Hitler Youth Stadium in Nuremberg. Here, Adolf Hitler had delivered his incendiary anti-Semitic speeches at the annual Nazi rallies. Now, four months after Germany's surrender and Hitler's suicide, American troops had painted over the swastikas, laid out a baseball diamond, and transformed the Fuhrer's platform for bigotry into a showcase of democratic ideals.

Baseball had swept through Europe that summer with the advance of American troops and the defeat of the Axis powers. Each military branch and its different divisions had their own teams. All told, more than 200,000 American servicemen played baseball across the Continent, which culminated in the European Theater of Operations championship, better known as the GI World Series. A month before the Detroit Tigers would play the Chicago Cubs back home, the Overseas Invasion Service Expedition (OISE) All-Stars based in France took on the heavily favored "Red Circlers" (so named for the patch on their uniform shoulders) representing the 71st Division of General George Patton's Third Army occupying Germany.

The St. Louis Cardinals' peacetime center fielder, Private First-Class "Harry the Hat" Walker (from his habit of adjusting his cap between pitches), had received a Bronze Star and Purple Heart for his wartime work as a reconnaissance scout. He also served as head of Germany's baseball operations. There, he had assembled a team for the playoffs from other units that included nine major leaguers on his 20-man roster. They included Cincinnati Reds pitcher Ewell Blackwell, who had gone undefeated and thrown a no-hitter in the playoffs leading up to the GI Series, and Pittsburgh Pirates outfielders Johnny Wyrostek and Maurice Van Robays.

Walker's nemesis in the opposite dugout for the championship was player-manager Staff Sergeant Sam Nahem, who had pitched two seasons in "The Show"—one with the Cardinals, one with the Phillies—then enlisted in the fall of 1942. Nahem had spent two years stateside before being sent overseas in late 1944, serving with an antiaircraft artillery unit. Nahem had been born to Syrian immigrants in a Jewish enclave of Brooklyn. He had quit college when Casey Stengel signed him to play in the Dodgers organization, doing his undergraduate studies and then law school during the off-seasons and passing the bar in New York. His eyeglasses bolstered his image as an intellectual, and so did quotes from Shakespeare and Maupassant he dropped in casual conversations.

At 6-foot-1 and 190 pounds (when the average man stood 5-foot-8), Nahem had physical size to match his intellect. But he had lacked the resources to assemble a team equal to Walker's, fielding a collection of semi-pro and minor-league players, plus one other major leaguer, Russ Bauers, a right-handed pitcher with a 29–29 record for the Pirates between 1936 and 1941. Nahem's best off-field move proved to be adding two Negro League stars at a time when the military's stark racial divisions prevented servicemen like Jackie Robinson and Larry Doby from playing baseball at their U.S. bases.

In the 1930s, Nahem had joined the Communist Party, which advocated for the abolition of Jim Crow and the integration of Organized Baseball. He integrated his OISE team with pitcher Leon Day of the Newark Eagles and the 818th Amphibious Battalion, a segregated unit. Day had driven a "duck," an amphibious vehicle, to deliver supplies on Utah Beach six days after D-Day, and outdueled Satchel Paige in the 1942 Negro League East-West All-Star Game. The other Negro League addition was power-hitting outfielder Willard Brown of the Kansas City Monarchs, whom Josh Gibson had nicknamed "Home Run Brown." Brown had entered the U.S. Army in 1944 and done his part in the D-Day invasion by hauling ammunition and guarding prisoners.

The first game of the Series, played that sunny Sunday afternoon in the Nuremberg stadium before 50,000 fans—easily the largest baseball crowd in Europe during the war—exposed the discrepancies between the two teams. Ewell "The Whip" Blackwell baffled the OISE batters with his side-armed, buggy whip delivery, striking out nine, while Nahem's fielders made seven errors behind him, and the Red Circlers waltzed to a 9–2 victory.

But the following afternoon, Leon Day—able to mix a killer curveball with 95-mph fastballs using his signature no windup, short-arm delivery—evened the series with an even more dominating performance than Blackwell's: striking out one more than "The Whip" (10 total) and allowing one less hit (four). Nahem, playing first base, produced two hits and drove in the winning run in the 2–1 triumph.

With the Series tied at one apiece, the two teams traveled to Reims, France, to play the next two games at Headquarters Command Athletic Field. On September 6, Nahem and Blackwell went at it again. Nahem had learned a slider from Burleigh Grimes, his manager in Montreal in 1939, which he used effectively. He also threw overhand to left-handed batters and side-arm to righties, which worked that day. Nahem allowed only four hits, one more than Blackwell, but his team prevailed in the runs column, winning 2–1 and giving the underdogs the Series lead.

In Game Four the next afternoon, Day could not repeat his magic of his previous start and was beaten 5–0. Walker hit a two-run home run while Day's team managed only five singles.

The decisive Game Five was played back in Nuremberg on September 8. Once again, Blackwell and Nahem took the mound for their respective teams. The Red Circlers took an early 1–0 lead. In the fourth inning with only one out, they loaded the bases. Nahem replaced himself on the mound with Bobby Keane and moved to first base. Keane retired the first two batters he faced to work out of the jam.

The Red Circlers tied the game in the sixth. In a dramatic bottom of the ninth inning, Nahem's team managed to push another run across the plate to seal a 2–1 win and the 1945 GI World Series victory.

Brigadier General Charles Thrasher honored the team back in France with a parade and a steak and champagne banquet. Rob Weintraub, who describes the moment in his book *The Victory Season*, notes, "Day and Brown, who would not be allowed to eat with their teammates in many major-league towns, celebrated alongside their fellow soldiers."

After the war, Nahem played on the weekends for a couple of years with the semipro Brooklyn Bushwicks and worked as a law clerk before the Phillies summoned him to pitch in 1948, mostly in relief. Worse than playing for a last-place team was playing under manager Ben Chapman, a noted bigot and anti-Semite. Nahem played another season with the Bushwicks and briefly in Puerto Rico before retiring. He found work with a fertilizer plant in California. Disillusioned by Russia, he left the Communist Party in 1957 but remained a social activist and union member for 25 years in his second career.

Brown returned to the Monarchs in 1946 and had his best season. The St. Louis Browns signed him midway through the 1947 season. He became the first Black man to hit a home run in the American League—a pinch-hit, inside-the-parker off Hal Newhouser—but the Browns released him after a month. He played two more seasons with the Monarchs and several for the Santurce Cangrejeros (Crabbers) in the Puerto Rican winter league, winning its Triple Crown twice. A special committee elected Brown posthumously to the National Baseball Hall of Fame in 2006.

There's a story—unconfirmed—that Jackie Robinson tried to convince Day to play with him in Montreal, so they could integrate Organized Baseball together in 1946, but Day opted instead to return to his old team in Newark. He pitched a no-hitter on Opening Day and helped his team win the Negro League World Series. Despite arm trouble, he pitched several more seasons in the Caribbean and the minor leagues before having to retire. On March 8, 1995—five days before his death from complications of diabetes and heart trouble—Day took a call in his hospital bed informing him that the Veterans Committee had elected him to the Hall of Fame. "I'm so happy, I don't know what to do," he said. "I never thought it would come."

Each one of these men had their moments of glory elsewhere, but it was united as teammates during the 1945 GI World Series that two Black men and the Jewish manager/pitcher/first baseman staged an upset not only of their opponents on the field but of the Nuremberg stadium's legacy in an extraordinary exhibition of equality.

Postscript

Two years earlier, another GI World Series had been contested in Algiers during October 1943 between the Casablanca Yankees and the Algiers Streetwalkers, composed of servicemen stationed in North Africa—medics for the Yankees and MPs for the Streetwalkers. The action was broadcast over Armed Forces Radio Network throughout the Mediterranean and covered by *Armed Forces Weekly* and the *Stars and Stripes*. The Casablanca Yankees, who swept the best two-of-three series, received a trophy made from an unexploded Italian bomb and baseballs autographed by General Dwight D. Eisenhower.

THE GREATEST COMEBACK OF ALL TIME

Tigers slugger Hank Greenberg paved the way for baseball stars to return to the majors after World War II.

MEMORIES & DREAMS, FALL 2009

Introduction

Hank Greenberg returned from his military service to active duty on the baseball diamond before most of his counterparts, which made him the test case to see if it could be done.

On July 1, 1945, Hank Greenberg stepped to the plate in the bottom half of the eighth inning wanting to prove that he could still play ball. The Tigers' 34-year-old left fielder had not played—except for one exhibition—since he entered the military in May 1941. Discharged only two weeks earlier as an Army Air Forces captain decorated with four battle stars, Greenberg had blistered the skin off his left hand taking batting practice to prepare for his return to the big leagues.

Throughout his four years stationed at bases in the United States and launching B-29 missions over the Himalayas in the China–Burma–India theater, Greenberg had dreamed about this day. But he was already 0-for-3. Nobody had attempted a return to baseball after such a long hiatus. Cynics doubted he would succeed. He, too, had wondered if he could regain his prewar form. In his last full season (1940), Greenberg had been the American League MVP, leading the league in doubles (50), homers (41), and RBIs (150) while batting .340. Digging into the batter's box, he felt upon him the eyes of the 47,729 fans swelling Briggs Stadium, turned out for the Tigers' afternoon doubleheader against the Philadelphia Athletics.

The Tigers' largest crowd of the season so far wanted to see Greenberg succeed. With some 500 MLB players serving in the military from 1941 to 1945, baseball fans had wearied of the subpar play by their one-armed, underage, and underachieving replacements. Seven weeks after Germany's surrender and only five weeks before Japan's, baseball fans wanted the Tigers' onetime star to let them know that the players' return demonstrated that the war was nearly over and the national pastime would be restored to its previous honor.

Greenberg, whose $55,000 salary had been the highest in baseball, also felt the pressure to perform from his peers. In the days leading to his return, the Associated Press's Whitney Martin had written: "He will be watched as a symbol of hope to all the other ballplayers in the service who fear their absence from the game might impair their effectiveness and money-earning capacity."

All that hung on the pitch approaching Greenberg at the plate. He uncoiled his bat and connected with a meaty *crack!* The ball sailed deep into the left-field bleachers. More than 47,000 fans rose in a mighty cheer. Odysseus had returned, and Penelope rejoiced.

*   *   *

The Tigers' sweep on July 1 increased their first-place lead over the Yankees to three and a half games. Four days later, Greenberg pinch-hit in the bottom of the ninth with two out, runners on second and third, and his team trailing the Red Sox 8–7. Greenberg singled to center, driving in two runs and putting the Tigers four and a half games up on the Yankees. Detroit had lost the 1944 pennant to the St. Louis Browns on the last day of the season, but with Greenberg back in 1945, they stood poised to win it.

Other vets followed Greenberg back to the majors, sparking the 1945 season with highlights. Bob Shepard, a left-handed minor-league pitcher prior to the war, lost his right leg after his fighter plane was shot down in

Germany. Still a lieutenant in the Army Air Forces rehabbing at Walter Reed Army Hospital, he coached the Washington Senators and—pressed into duty on August 4 to throw five and a half innings of relief (allowing only three hits and one run)—became the first leg amputee to pitch in the majors.

Toronto-born pitcher Dick Fowler returned to the Athletics on September 9 from serving in the Canadian Army to hurl a no-hitter against the Browns at Shibe Park in his first start in three years.

The Indians' Bob Feller came back from nearly four years in the navy to face the Tigers in a night game at Cleveland on August 24. The USS *Alabama*'s former gun captain fanned 12 batters—including Greenberg twice—in a four-hit, 4–2 win. Rapid Robert, a 25-game winner in 1941, would pitch nine games for the Indians through the rest of the campaign, finishing 5–3 with a 2.50 ERA.

With the loss to Feller, the Tigers' first-place lead dropped to a half-game over the Washington Senators. Going into the final day of the regular season, September 30, Detroit needed to win at least one game of a double-header against the St. Louis Browns at Sportsman's Park. Rain delayed the start of the first game Sunday afternoon and continued to fall occasionally once play finally started, slicking the grass and muddying the basepaths.

Greenberg approached the plate in the ninth with the bases loaded, one out, and his team behind 3–2. The ex–Army Air Forces captain had slugged a dozen home runs in the three months since his return and batted .309, but he had gone 1-for-4 in this critical game and ended an earlier rally when he was picked off third base. If he failed at bat here, he would seal his place as the game's goat.

With a light mist falling, Greenberg rubbed a hunk of bone against the handle of his bat. He settled his spikes in the dirt and watched the first pitch miss the plate. He turned on the next pitch, a screwball, and sent it deep down the left-field line. The crowd knew instantly the ball had the distance to win the game if it stayed fair—and it did. Greenberg had capped his return with a grand slam to win the pennant! "Never was a title won in more dramatic fashion," the *New York Times* reported six years before Bobby Thomson would hit his shot heard 'round the world.

*   *   *

Nearly two months after V-J Day, the first postwar World Series opened in Detroit on a chilly Wednesday afternoon in October. Ex–army sergeant Joe Louis was on hand only days after his discharge from 44 months in the service to watch his beloved Tigers. The world heavyweight champ who "would rather discuss Hank Greenberg and the Tigers" than boxing, according to the *New York Times*, watched the Chicago Cubs rough up Detroit's Hal Newhouser en route to a 9–0 rout.

The following afternoon, Hank Greenberg took matters into his own hands. In the first inning, the Tigers' left fielder cut down the Cubs' Stan Hack, trying to score from second on a single, with a perfect peg to the plate. Four innings later, with the score tied 1–1, Greenberg blasted a three-run shot deep into the left-field stands that powered the Tigers' 4–1 win.

Afterward in the Detroit clubhouse with his teammates still congratulating him, Greenberg refused to pose for a photo without winning pitcher Virgil Trucks. The husky, hard-throwing right-hander had pitched a complete game, yielding only seven hits, in only his second start since March 22, 1944, when he had entered the navy. Trucks's first start after his recent release had come on the final day of the regular season in the game Greenberg had won with his grand slam. The two vets turned World Series stars posed in a bear hug for the AP photographer in the Tigers clubhouse.

The Cubs took the final game in Detroit to return home with a 2–1 lead in the Series, but the Tigers won Game Four at Wrigley, helped by Greenberg's hit that drove in the game's first run. Hal Newhouser, Detroit's southpaw ace and AL MVP who had faltered in the first game, started Game Five and showed the stuff that had won him the pitcher's Triple Crown—leading the league in wins (25), ERA (1.81), and strikeouts (212)—during the regular season. The Tigers won 8–4. Greenberg hit three doubles and scored three runs; the Tigers took a 3–2 lead in the Series.

Monday afternoon, the Cubs chased Game Two star Virgil Trucks in the fifth with a four-run rally. The Tigers clawed back with a four-run rally of their own, completed by Greenberg's solo homer to tie the game 7–7. The score remained knotted into the bottom of the 12th when Chicago's Hack tagged a ball to left field. Greenberg came in to play the ball on the bounce, but it hopped over his head. The runner from first scored to give the Cubs the win, 8–7, and to even the Series. (The three official scorers initially charged Greenberg with an error, but after criticism from the press box, Tigers clubhouse, and the Cubs' manager, the scorers reversed the decision to a hit in an unprecedented move.)

That left the 1945 Series to be decided by one game on Tuesday afternoon, October 9, at Wrigley Field. The Tigers turned to Newhouser with only two days' rest. The Tigers' pitcher had been classified 4-F because of a leaky heart valve, but that hadn't stopped him from trying to enlist several times—only to be turned down each time. The Tiger lefty showed his heart, striking out 10 in Detroit's 9–3 win.

The Tigers had satisfied baseball fans with a seven-game World Series victory, and for stars like Ted Williams, Joe DiMaggio, and Stan Musial who would leave the battleground for the ball field the following season (1946), Hank Greenberg had promised hope for their return to glory with his successful comeback.

Postscript

Greenberg played two more years, retiring after the 1947 season at age 36. I elaborate on Greenberg's return from military service and tell the rest of his story in my biography *Hank Greenberg: The Hero of Heroes* (2013).

OPENING DAY: 1946

Before it could heal the nation, baseball at the close of World War II had some healing of its own to do.

HISTORY CHANNEL MAGAZINE, MAY/JUNE 2003

Introduction

I was glad to get to know Jim Tarbox when he was editing the *History Channel Magazine* because, among other reasons, he was a baseball fan and let me write several articles about the game's history—like this one.

On Tuesday, April 16, 1946, the president of the United States lunched with several U.S. senators at the Capitol, paused to shake hands with wounded war veterans, then headed to the ballpark. A 65-piece U.S. Army band boomed "Hail to the Chief" when Harry S. Truman entered Griffith Stadium. The ballplayers—13 of them returning vets—stood at attention in their baggy flannels while the band continued with the national anthem and the Stars and Stripes rose up the center-field pole.

The photographers trained their bulky cameras on the presidential box, where the commander in chief would honor the game's great south-paws with his opening toss. Truman caused a moment of consternation by gripping the ball in his right hand. The *New York Herald Tribune* reported: "He switched the ball to the publicized duke, limbered it up with two short waves of the soupbone, drew it back behind his ear, and fired an overhand delivery about 50 feet into the cluster of players of both sides deploying for the throw."

Truman's pitch was the first season-opening delivery by the commander in chief since Franklin Delano Roosevelt's in April 1941, but Opening Day was more than a photo op for Truman. When the war ended, the President turned to the national pastime for healing. The Missouri southpaw understood the nation's faith in the game's restorative powers.

*   *   *

Washington's Griffith Stadium had been sold out weeks in advance, and eager fans quickly snatched up the 4,000 bleacher seats and 3,000 standing-room-only passes that went on sale that morning. Some 32,300 men, women, and children filled the seats and spilled into the aisles to watch that afternoon's game between the Boston Red Sox and the hometown Senators. Across the country, 236,730 fans passed through the turnstiles at eight American and National League parks, the highest inaugural-day attendance in 15 years.

The ballpark turnstiles would keep spinning throughout 1946. That year, attendance leaped to 18.5 million—a 71 percent gain from the 10.8 million in 1945 and the largest jump from one year to the next in baseball history. After following the war campaign on European soil and in the Pacific theater, Americans were eager to turn their attention to peacetime diversions.

"People confronted by this awful thing which jarred their minds had to recover," says John Rossi, author of *A Whole New Game: Off the Field Changes in Baseball 1946–1960*. "One of the ways you recover is to embrace all of those things that were traditional and normal from your past."

Seizing upon this, Major League Baseball enticed customers with the ad campaign "The Stars Are Back." The American public answered the call to see Ted Williams, Joe DiMaggio, Stan Musial, Bill Dickey, Pee Wee Reese, and others. *The Sporting News* observed, "With the return of many diamond stars from military service during the past year, the majors' 1946 opening-day lineups not only took on a new luster, but also resembled more closely the first-day arrays of 1941—the last prewar campaign—than did any of the past three inaugurals."

The summer of 1941, when Williams batted .406 and DiMaggio hit safely in 56 straight games, had been baseball's finest as far as anyone could remember. With the stars back, the fans longed for a return to the game's glory days.

After the December 1941 bombing of Pearl Harbor, baseball commissioner Kenesaw Landis wired FDR that baseball was his to command. The President declared the game must go on. With the war effort demanding longer hours, he reasoned, workers deserved the game's entertainment. "I honestly feel that it would be best for the country to keep baseball going," FDR wrote back in his famous "Green Light Letter."

But the game suffered from the war-thinned ranks. More than 500 major leaguers either enlisted or were drafted into military service, replaced by 4-Fs and ill-qualified opportunists. The Cincinnati Reds let 15-year-old Joe Nuxhall take the mound in 1944. The kid gave up five runs in 2/3 of an inning, exiting the game with a 67.50 ERA. Pete Gray, who had lost his right arm in a boyhood accident, played right field for the St. Louis Browns in 1945. Over-the-hill stars put retirement on hold, and marginal players who might have been invited for a cup of coffee in the bigs during ordinary times stayed for breakfast, lunch, and dinner. Eddie Basinski, an accomplished concert violinist, proved to be only a mediocre middle infielder for the 1945 Dodgers.

By the end of 1945, Major League Baseball had sunk to a new low, and the 1945 World Series was called the worst ever: "the fat men against the tall men at the office picnic," according to Geoffrey C. Ward and Ken Burns in their 1994 book *Baseball: An Illustrated History.* Even though wartime travel restrictions forced its cancellation, the All-Star Game's absence in 1945 served as fitting commentary on the game's paucity of talent. Baseball looked to the returning stars—hoping their skills were still sharp—to save the game.

* * *

The Washington starter, knuckleballer Roger Wolff, threw the game's first pitch to Red Sox leadoff hitter Dominic DiMaggio. Nicknamed "The Little Professor," Dominic was smaller than brother Joe, one of only a few ballplayers who wore glasses, and maintained a professorial vocabulary even on the field. He had spent three years in the U.S. Navy. Wolff, a freak 20-game winner in 1945, retired the Boston side, including Ted Williams. In the second, the Red Sox nicked Wolff for a run, and Williams returned to bat in the third. President Truman watched closely as "The Splendid Splinter" dug in on the left side of the plate and worked the count to 3–2.

Truman, along with the rest of America, wanted to see if Williams after the war was as good as he'd been before it. Throughout the extra-long spring training that year—when managers weighed emerging talents of select replacement players against the rusty skills of returning servicemen—Williams endured the oft-repeated question: After three years as a navy pilot, could he return to his earlier dominant batting form? He answered them all on Opening Day.

On the 3–2 pitch, Williams uncoiled his familiar, sweet swing. The Kid's slight uppercut rocketed the ball 440 feet into the dead-center stands, the longest homer hit in Griffith Stadium since Lou Gehrig belted a similar blast 15 years earlier. When Williams crossed home plate, the President gave him a grin and a tip of the hat.

In their half of the third, the Senators squeezed out a run on three singles against Boston right-hander Tex Hughson, making his first start since spending 1945 in the army. Williams mitigated the damage when he caught a long drive at the left-field wall, slugged by the Senators' cleanup hitter Cecil Travis. The shortstop had hit .359 in 1941, finishing second to Williams. But he had suffered frostbite in December 1944 in the Battle of the Bulge as an infantryman with the 76th Division. Travis would struggle to hit .252 in 1946 and retire at 34 after the next season, when he batted only .216—his baseball career a casualty of the war, as much from consuming his youth as from freezing his feet. Boston added a run in the fifth, increasing its lead to 3–1 when DiMaggio drove in catcher Hal Wagner, but left fielder Jeff Heath homered in Washington's half of the sixth. The President again doffed his hat; his Senators had pulled within a run at 3–2.

* * *

Along with the other thousands of fans on hand, Truman welcomed the game's diversion from the nation's troubles. The brief recession caused by industrial reversion—from tanks to cars, from mosquito netting to shirts—had triggered fears of the Depression's return. Warnings of "extreme inflationary danger" from Office of Economic Stabilization spokesman Chester Bowles justified continued wage and price controls. Furthermore, the government was reimposing wartime controls on meat and dairy products in an effort to curb world famine.

Truman had already weathered complaints over delays in bringing the soldiers home. Once stateside, vets still couldn't get to their actual homes because the existing transportation system was overwhelmed. After his discharge at Bainbridge, Maryland, in March 1946, Stan Musial—the 1944 National League batting champ—caught a train to Philadelphia but couldn't find room on a bus out of town, so he hitchhiked the rest of the way home. Although he missed part of spring training, Musial went on to become the National League's Most Valuable Player in 1946. The Chicago

White Sox offered a season pass to anyone providing a lead that resulted in housing for 20 team members who had nowhere to live on Opening Day.

Meanwhile, paranoia about communism was mounting, crime was on the rise, and racial tensions were surging. In this milieu, Americans—from the President to the factory worker—embraced baseball. "Baseball was a place of relief," says Robert Maddox, professor emeritus of American history at Penn State University. "You go from your lousy job to this ballpark with grass—no turf—and cheer for a couple of hours. It was as much escapism as the motion pictures were then."

The hometown fans had little to cheer when the Sox scored three in the top of the seventh. Johnny Pesky figured in all three runs. The swift-footed shortstop doubled to drive in Wagner and DiMaggio then scored himself on Bobby Doerr's single. Pesky had been in Pearl Harbor, poised to ship out to Okinawa when Truman decided to drop the bombs that ended the war. "I was just so darn glad to get back to playing ball," Pesky, now 83, recalls. "In those years, we didn't make a lot of money, but we paid our bills."

Not everyone could say the same. The cost of living in 1946 had risen 18 percent over 1945, yet management refused raises until price controls were dropped. Labor rebelled. Unions had gained strength during the war, and they unleashed the largest strike wave in U.S. history. By the time Wolff took the mound for the Senators, electrical workers, metalworkers, meat cutters, steelworkers, tugboat operators, autoworkers, and mine workers had all organized strikes. Throughout the course of the year, an estimated 5 million workers would walk off the job.

*   *   *

Baseball reflected the nation's conditions. Many players expected raises after the war that weren't forthcoming. Danny Gardella, for instance, hit 18 home runs for the New York Giants in 1945 while making $4,500. The next year he was offered an additional $500, which he didn't think was enough.

Until then, players either signed or sought another line of work. Baseball's reserve clause bound a player to a club until management released, sold, or traded him, which effectively eliminated a player's leverage in negotiations. As a result, Jorge Pasquel, president of the Mexican League, accused Major League Baseball of running a "slave market" and further claimed that Organized Baseball was an illegal monopoly. In 1946 Pasquel and his brothers, who had amassed a fortune estimated between $20 and $60 million in land, cattle, and customs brokering, offered to liberate American players—for example, by paying the likes of Gardella $15,000.

Owners of American teams feared an exodus, especially after reports that the Pasquels had offered Musial, who was making $13,500 for the St. Louis Cardinals, a $50,000 contract. At that time, only six major leaguers made more than $25,000. After the Pasquels reportedly offered Williams and Feller each $100,000, Commissioner Albert Benjamin "Happy" Chandler, Landis's successor, decreed that any player who jumped his contract would be banned from playing Major League Baseball for five years.

With labor unrest rampant and the Mexican League a bargaining chip, Harvard lawyer Robert Murphy figured the time was right for baseball players to join the organized labor movement. Two days before Truman's ceremonial toss, Murphy registered the American Baseball Guild as an independent union.

Murphy nearly pulled off baseball's first strike on June 7, 1946. In a closed two-hour meeting, the Pittsburgh Pirates voted 20–16 not to take the field for that afternoon's game against the New York Giants. But that was four votes short of the two-thirds minimum required to strike.

Prompted by the Mexican League threat and Murphy's rabblerousing, the owners finally agreed to negotiate with player representatives in a series of meetings that summer to improve working conditions. The owners did not revoke the reserve clause but, among other concessions, they set a $5,000 minimum salary (at the time, 50 players earned less than that per season).

One writer heralded the new agreement as baseball's Magna Carta, but celebrated baseball scribe Red Smith took a more cynical view. "In Pittsburgh, where organizational work was farthest advanced, the club is pleading that unionization would be 'completely destructive of the game of baseball,'" Smith wrote. "There never has been a child labor law proposed whose opponents didn't bleat that it would destroy their business."

The strike wave in 1946 would lead to the passing of the Taft-Hartley Act the following year, which diminished the unions' power. But Organized Baseball's first union effort in 1946 would lay the groundwork for the Major League Baseball Players Association, formed eight seasons later.

*   *   *

Race colored postwar labor issues. Blacks who had filled in as replacement workers found themselves suddenly unemployed when returning servicemen resumed their jobs under provisions of the GI Bill. And Blacks who had served their country also lost ground when they returned home. "Black soldiers came back expecting more privilege but not getting it," says Maddox.

In 1946, Truman created a Committee on Civil Rights to investigate racial abuses. It called for anti-lynching legislation and an end to segregated housing. That year, nine Black men were lynched in the United States and another 21 were rescued from angry mobs.

Opening Day at Griffith Stadium reflected the times. If you look closely at the photos, everyone wearing flannels—on the field, in the dugout, in the bullpen—is white. Not one Black player, despite the abundant talent in the Negro Leagues.

Major League Baseball had banned Blacks—covertly and overtly. Although no record exists of a secret vote by the owners, Commissioner Chandler and Brooklyn Dodgers co-owner Branch Rickey maintained that the owners voted 15–1 in 1946 to not allow Blacks in the big leagues, with Rickey casting the lone vote in favor. Three years earlier, Commissioner Landis had blocked the Pirates' effort to sign legendary Black slugger Josh Gibson. Following Landis's death in 1944, however, Chandler expressed an attitude altered by the war: "If a Black boy can make it on Okinawa and Guadalcanal, hell, he can make it in baseball."

So it was that two days after the lily-white Opening Day at Griffith Stadium, Jackie Robinson, the grandson of a slave, hurdled Organized Baseball's color barrier when he took the field for the Montreal Royals in their first game of the season. In his debut for the Dodgers' AAA affiliate, Robinson collected four hits, including a three-run homer, stole two bases, and provoked two balks that twice sent him home from third. Throughout 1946, Robinson riveted baseball fans' attention on his Montreal season. After he led the Royals to victory in the minor-league World Series, adoring fans chased him for three blocks through Montreal's streets. "It was probably the only day in history that a Black man ran from a white mob with love instead of lynching on its mind," one of Robinson's friends later observed.

The next year, Robinson would start at first base for Brooklyn on Opening Day. Even though *The Sporting News* would name Robinson its Rookie of the Year, respect from other players—many of them from the rural South—would come only slowly and begrudgingly. Still, Robinson and Rickey permanently changed the complexion of the national pastime.

"You can almost divide American history in the 20th century into before Robinson and after Robinson," writer Gerard Early reflects. "America was defined by baseball. This was our national game. So the drama of this moment of Robinson coming in is enormous because of the game being tied to the national character—in some way the game being tied to America's sense of its mission and its destiny."

In the bottom of the ninth, the home team trailed 6–2. Senators second baseman Gerald Priddy doubled off Hughson, and catcher Al Evans drove him in. President Truman had stood for the ritual seventh-inning stretch with the rest of baseball's faithful. Now he was prepared to stay for extra innings should Washington manage to tie the game. He had munched popcorn and sipped a soda from a paper cup. Now it seemed he didn't want his day at the ballpark to end. But the Sox squashed the Senators' rally, and Opening Day was over.

Americans yearned for a return to normalcy, but the issues that tormented baseball in 1946—labor disputes and racial integration—were the very issues that confronted the nation. For the President, that meant it was back to work at the office after a pleasant diversion at the ballpark.

Postscript

The Red Sox also figured prominently in the final game of the season, Game Seven of the World Series. Heavily favored to win the Series, the Red Sox had split the first six games with the Cardinals. With the score tied 3–3 in the bottom of the eighth, two out, and Enos Slaughter on first, the Cardinals' Harry Walker lined a base hit to left-center. Slaughter took off, ran past the third-base coach's stop sign, and headed home. Red Sox shortstop Johnny Pesky took the relay throw, pivoted, and hesitated for an instant before throwing home—too late. Slaughter's run proved the difference, sealing the Sox' defeat 4–3.

Chapter 3

PERSONALITIES

THE LEGEND OF LA TORTUGA

Willians Astudillo is a utility infielder for the Minnesota Twins. And a cult hero. How did that happen?

CITY PAGES, MAY 2019

Introduction

At the close of the 2018 season, a phenomenon began that carried over into 2019. Call it "Turtle fever." Twins fans were smitten by an obsession for a flamboyant yet media-shy backup from Venezuela. I wanted to find out what beguiled them so and who this guy was.

This is not just any Friday night at Target Field. It's "An Evening with La Tortuga."

The Twins expected 2,000 fans to take them up on the offer of a ticket to the April 26 game against the Orioles and a Tortuga T-shirt. Demand was so high they had to print another 1,000 shirts—which promptly sold out.

In the stands above the home team dugout, a 10-year-old boy in a Twins cap watches the players filing off the field as batting practice winds down. Nelson Cruz passes by. Eddie Rosario. Byron Buxton. The boy doesn't flinch. Finally he spots Willians Astudillo. He holds up a drawing of a green turtle and calls, "Tortuga!"

Astudillo stops. The boy tosses him a ball and pen. Astudillo signs the ball and several more for other boys who quickly gather before he heads into the clubhouse. The boys reverently regard his autograph.

Up on the concourse along the third-base side, a father walks with his 11-year-old son, both wearing black La Tortuga shirts: a red No. 64 over a beige turtle shell on the back and the meme of Astudillo running on the front. Matt Guttman introduces his son Zach: "This is his biggest fan."

Last summer, they attended the Twins' final game—not to say good-bye to the old star, Joe Mauer, but to meet the new one. Matt pulls out his phone and flashes a photo. In it, La Tortuga leans into the stands, smiling with his new bestie, Zach.

Matt had the photo made into an 8" × 10" print, and when they heard Astudillo would be at Fan HQ in the Mall of America the previous weekend, they road-tripped there from their Plymouth (Minnesota) home. Matt shows another image on his phone of Astudillo signing the photo. They would not have missed this evening.

"He's fun to watch," says Zach, who plays baseball himself: third base, pitcher, outfield. "All over, kind of like him."

Like many fans, Zach loves the guy. At the same time, he marvels at his quick rise to celebrity: "He doesn't even have 200 at-bats in his [MLB] career, but is already having a theme night."

Indeed, 142 at-bats, for those keeping score at home, and already he has not only a theme night, but a drink (La Tortuga Cocktail, served at Bat & Barrel and Town Ball Tavern) and a sandwich (La Tortuga Torta, served at a sandwich cart behind section 114) named after him. Astudillo T-shirts have sold more than any other Twins'. His highlights go viral more frequently than Rosario goes yard, which has made him an instant social media sensation and cult hero.

Astudillo has become the team's most popular player faster than anybody in Twins history, yet he's not even a regular starter. He's a newbie to the majors, a journeyman minor leaguer, a 27-year-old utility fielder the marketing department esteems more than the manager, who hasn't had the confidence to pencil him into the starting lineup this evening. Having a theme night for Willians Astudillo is like feting Jerry Terrell, retiring Al Newman's number, or hosting a Nick Punto party. How did we get here?

*   *   *

Rocco Baldelli's decision to have Astudillo start his evening on the bench enraged La Tortuga's legions. The way they lit up social media with their frustration made it look like another Arab Spring. Their passion for him mirrors the passion he displays on the field. He's captured their hearts. You see them post comments like "It's not always easy to be positive about the Twins, but I love that guy," from md56482. "The most compelling player the Twins have had in many years," LoisMA. "Another reason why baseball is great," Blake R., and "I love this man," Margo L.

They call him the most talented Twin. A Hall of Famer. The GOAT. Obviously blinded by love, but forgive them. It's been a long time since a player excited Twins Nation this much. We loved Kirby, of course. But he let us down with his dark side. Eddie Guardado had the spark but took nearly 10 years to catch fire. Torii Hunter was lovable but left. Going further back, Killebrew was too even keeled. There's simply never been a Twins player fans have fallen for so hard so fast.

The first thing you see when you look at Willians Astudillo is, well, his body. At 5-foot-9, 225 pounds, he looks more like a bowling pin than a professional baseball player. You might say, politely, he's stocky. Husky. Chunky. Short for his weight. Could be the love child of Jack Black and Amy Schumer. A Prince Fielder mini-me. Bluto with a bat.

Which makes him all the more irresistible. The fan in the stands snarfing nachos from a plastic batting helmet or the guy on the couch at home with beer in hand looks at Astudillo and sees himself. "He doesn't look like your typical ballplayer," says Matt Guttman, who's about Astudillo's height yet slender. "He gives a lot of people hope you don't have to be 6'2" and 250 pounds to succeed."

Combine that with a rubbery face as flexible and expressive as Al Schacht's framed by a mullet perm that'd be tops in any of John King's hockey hair videos, and talent that pops up all over the field, and you've got the makings of baseball highlight porn. Here's a quick tour:

The moment that got him noticed happened at spring training last year. From behind the plate, Astudillo catches the pitch and—without leaving his crouch or shifting his gaze from the pitcher—whips the ball to first base to pick off the runner, who doesn't know what's happened.

Playing third at Rochester in August, Astudillo fields a throw with a runner reaching the base and simply pockets the ball in his glove. When the pitcher climbs the mound, and the runner takes his lead, Astudillo pounces on him with the tag. Another runner out and left wondering, WTF?

Astudillo auditioned for the outfield with a clip he sent to Twins brass of him in center field during the 2014–15 Venezuelan winter league season. He runs back to the wall, sets, jumps—well, more hops; he doesn't really get much air—and nabs the ball before it disappears over the fence to deny a home run. He lands flat on his belly, rolls to his side, and raises his glove to show a clean catch—more seal performing a trick than Gold Glover.

In another fielding blooper converted into an out, this one while catching for the Twins last summer, Astudillo scampers from behind the plate to field a bunt, snaps a throw to third, collides with Jose Berrios coming off the mound, and falls flush on his face. That's another reason he's so entertaining—he can inject slapstick into the routine.

In a braver moment behind the plate this past April in Philadelphia, Astudillo stands his ground with the ball while Bryce Harper bears down on him. Harper tries to hurdle the Turtle but collides with him. Astudillo falls back, rolls once, comes to rest on his knees, and raises the ball in his right hand to show the ump, *I got him!* The ump pumps his fist. Out!

Astudillo hit a walk-off homer for the Twins against Kansas City on September 9, but it was his performance after a game-winning blast earlier this year in the Venezuelan playoffs that deserves the Oscar. He swings so hard he finishes on one knee then holds the pose, forearms crossed over the knob of his upright bat, and watches the ball sail toward the left-field pole. "I thought it was going foul," he said later. When he sees it stay fair, his enthusiasm carries him around the bases, past his teammates clumped at home, and through a routine of sideways jumping jacks the length of the dugout, exhorting cheers from the crowd. The clip's a combination of sublime cool and unrestrained joy

But the instant classic, the one that solidified the legend of La Tortuga, comes from September 12 at Target Field. Astudillo is on first when Max Kepler's hit to left-center eludes Yankees center fielder Aaron Hicks's dive. Astudillo rounds second and chugs for third. He sheds his helmet along the way—shades of Willie Mays in slow motion. He rounds third already gassed. With the throw from the outfield heading to the cutoff man, the drama plays out on Astudillo's eloquent face. He's grimacing, biting his tongue, willing the luggage of his body forward. His long curls unfurl behind him. He runs and runs and runs. He's gasping. A drowning man fighting for air. The throw reaches the cutoff man. And still Astudillo chugs on. Finally—finally!—longer than it took Odysseus to find his way home, La Tortuga slides in safely.

After much ribbing from teammates and manager Paul Molitor admitting, "That was painful to watch," Astudillo said, "I just wanted to show that chubby people also run."

So that became his tagline. It's on the front of the giveaway T-shirt, above the image of him on his mad dash over the words "RUN, RUN, RUN."

The personality that fueled his 270-foot run and his reply are infectious among fans and his teammates. Astudillo grew up choosing Nelson Cruz for home run contests playing MLB video games, yet he's brash enough to call the veteran "vieja" (old lady) in jest. Cruz retorts with "Señor Barriga" (Mr. Big Belly). "He gets mad at me," Cruz says, laughing. Before the game on La Tortuga Night, Cruz wears one of the black promo shirts along with a handful of teammates. "He's just fun to be around," he says. "Always positive. He brings good energy to the clubhouse."

Kyle Gibson agrees. He likes pitching to Astudillo—whom he calls "Torts"—and playing cards with him. "I'm on a pretty good streak of beating him in the card game Casino right now. I give him a hard time about that," Gibson says. "Because he's a young guy, he ends up being the brunt of some jokes. He also kind of brings it on himself and enjoys it a little bit. He likes to make jokes and take jokes at the same time. He's one of the guys who keeps it light around here."

He seems to inspire that sort of reaction in everyone. When asked to comment on Astudillo, Twins catching coach Bill Evers smiles reflexively. Why? "Because he brings that energy every day to the game," Evers says. "He's fun to watch because he plays with passion. He cares about what he does, and he puts the time and effort into it."

"I don't know how you can talk about him and not smile," Baldelli says in a taped television interview. He's smiling himself, his eyes gleaming. "He's a really enjoyable player to watch for a lot of reasons, but he's also a really talented guy. This is a guy who has a really unique ability with a bat in his hands."

He's talking about Astudillo's ability to make contact. The Turtle is a free swinger who seems to be able to hit the ball wherever it's thrown. Back in spring training, the BP pitcher was messing with him. He edged his pitches farther and farther outside. Astudillo kept getting his bat on them. Then he moved inside, closer and closer. Same thing—Astudillo swung and made contact. Finally, the pitcher tossed a ball *behind* Astudillo—who turned and whacked it with an axe stroke.

Astudillo figures he developed his hand-eye coordination as a boy when his father, a retired professional baseball player, flicked corn kernels in the backyard that Astudillo picked out of the air with the swing of a broomstick. Try that at home.

Through the end of April, he had the best contact rate in the majors. His 96.8 percent was way higher than the MLB average of 76.9 percent last year (meaning when batters swung, they made contact roughly three out of four times). That skill makes him an ideal pinch hitter or batter in hit-and-run situations.

His extraordinary hand-eye coordination means he almost never strikes out, an anomaly in this age of the inflated strikeout rate. In the minor leagues, he had the lowest strikeout rate among all double-A and triple-A players the past two years and among all minor-league players the two years before that. In 2,461 plate appearances throughout nine seasons, he struck out only 81 times, a measly 3.3 percent. (Anything under 10 percent is considered excellent.) In "The Show," he has become the batter least likely to strike out in major-league history, relative to the league. With five career home runs and four walks, he is the only MLB player with at least 150 plate appearances in the past century to have more home runs than strikeouts.

Astudillo likes to swing at the ball. He doesn't like to walk. Throughout his nine seasons in the minors, he walked as infrequently as he struck out, only 85 times or 3.5 percent of his plate appearances. He had not gotten to a 2–0 count in the majors until April 6 of this year.

When the next pitch is a ball, Twins television play-by-play man Dick Bremer observes, "Now three-and-oh to a man who's hard to walk."

"Probably a career high with three straight pitches taken," commentator Justin Morneau adds, chuckling.

The next pitch is a high fastball, slightly outside. He could take it—the way most batters would—for ball four and a free pass. But Astudillo, who has already bashed one home run that afternoon, swings big. Misses. And falls down.

Bremer laughs.

Astudillo fouls off the next pitch. Full count.

The Phillies pitcher delivers a 92-mph fastball inside at the knees. Astudillo backs away.

"Astudillo has drawn a walk," Bremer declares. "And what will be in the headlines in the newspaper tomorrow? A possible Twins win? Their three home runs? Or the fact that Astudillo has drawn a walk?!"

"All we need is a stolen base to top it off," Morneau cracks. (That would be another major-league first for La Tortuga, who comes by his nickname honestly.)

As SABRites worship at the altar of the "three true outcomes" (home runs, walks, and strikeouts), Astudillo is guilty of apostasy. Through the first month of the 2019 season, he had one walk and one strikeout. Plus two home runs. Here's yet another aspect of his appeal. Not only is he a maverick as a disciplined free swinger, he's also a free thinker in the batter's box.

* * *

Despite his life-of-the-party reputation, Astudillo is subdued and serious during a pregame interview in the dugout. He answers questions in Spanish that are translated by Elvis Martinez, the Twins' interpreter, to a reporter. Afterward, Martinez points out that Astudillo's businesslike manner is his standard MO with media. Astudillo came from nothing in the port town of Barcelona, Venezuela, and while he's working near the major-league minimum wage of $550,000 a year, he knows that if he doesn't make it, poverty awaits him.

The Turtle went at his own pace through the minors. Signed by the Phillies shortly after his 17th birthday, he spent three years in the Venezuelan summer league before winding his way through the Gulf Coast League, the South Atlantic League, and the Florida State League, only to be released by the Phillies in 2015. Signed by the Braves, he played a summer in the double-A Southern League and was released.

Winter ball in Venezuela seemed the only constant. Signed by the Diamondbacks, he batted .342 in the triple-A Pacific Coast League, but instead of being promoted, he got released. Again. The Twins signed him in November 2017 and sent him to Rochester in the triple-A International League. The man paid his dues, another credit in his favor among Twins fans with their midwestern work ethic.

When the Rochester manager told Astudillo in late June 2018 that the parent club had called and wanted him to join the team in Chicago, he was so excited, he telephoned his parents in Venezuela, even though it was late at night. He woke them up. They didn't believe him. Ten long years had passed since the major leagues had first expressed interest. They thought he was joking.

But it was true. In a game against the Cubs on June 30, Molitor sent Astudillo out to left field in the fifth inning to relieve Rosario on a very hot day. "I was extremely nervous, especially playing in Wrigley and in the outfield, not my natural position," he tells Kyle Gibson on his podcast *Meeting on the Mound*. "But it felt really good to be out there and in the big leagues and to show people what I can do." That included a single in his major-league debut at-bat, which drove in the tying run. He also caught two fly balls, made no errors. And so the legend began.

Even though he lasted only three weeks, Astudillo burnished the legend when he took the mound to finish out a game already lost to the Tampa Bay Rays. Astudillo, who had won a game the summer before pitching two scoreless innings for triple-A Reno, did not threaten the job security of anyone in the Twins bullpen. He gave up five runs, including a homer to the first batter he faced. But he appeared so overmatched—David pitching to Goliath yet persevering—that he won over the fans, who embraced him as the lovable underdog.

Astudillo is listed as a catcher, though it appears he can play anywhere (except maybe pitcher). Called up again in September, he played first, second, third, left field, center field, and catcher. This season, he has added right field to his résumé. That's led to speculation of him playing all nine positions in a game like fellow Venezuelan and Twin Cesar Tovar did in 1968. Molitor introduced the idea as a joke last year. Baldelli has toyed over it with reporters but recently insisted he would not be putting Astudillo at shortstop, the last position for him to check off the list.

Astudillo himself says he has no aspirations of following in Tovar's footsteps—though he insists he could, pointing to 10 years playing shortstop as a youth. He thought he was going to get his chance in spring training this year when he saw his name at short on the lineup card for the next day's game. He texted friend and countryman Ehire Adrianza, nervously asking for some helpful advice. But the assignment turned out to be a clerical error, and the next day Astudillo was at second, not short.

Still, he has proven his value with his versatility. This year and last he has appeared most often at the infield corners when he's not behind the plate—or on the bench. Through the Twins' first two dozen games, Astudillo had started only four games at catcher and 14 total, little more than half. Management does not seem to have complete confidence in him as a catcher, preferring the experience of Jason Castro, who had started 11 games behind the plate in the same span, or the promise of Mitch Garver, who started nine. Last year, in his first call-up, Molitor didn't use Astudillo at catcher once.

Catching coach Bill Evers notes that Astudillo has made progress as a catcher, is adapting to implementing the game plan, and is becoming more adept with his soft hands at framing pitches to win strikes. When asked, "Do you think catcher is his best position?" Evers replies, tellingly, "I think he is a wonderful utility man that brings energy all over the diamond and has the athleticism even though the body type does not [make you] think of a great athlete. He's an excellent athlete that can play other positions."

So don't expect Evers to be lobbying for Astudillo to assume the starting job behind the plate. General manager Derek Falvey has admitted, too, that he and his scouts haven't been quite sure how to best employ Astudillo's talents, which included a .320/.340/.531 line with two home runs and seven RBIs before a 10-day sabbatical on the injured list from late April into early May. La Tortuga defies standard models and current projection metrics. "There are not many [comparisons] for him," Falvey said during spring training.

* * *

That may explain why Astudillo's role on his special night has been limited to three brief cameos warming up the pitcher while starting catcher Mitch Garver straps on his gear. It's not until the bottom of the eighth inning, with the game seemingly in hand, that Baldelli gives the fans what they've paid to see.

When Astudillo is announced over the PA system to lead off, the fans applaud happily, sounding louder than the 15,000 or so there.

Inspired, La Tortuga goes all in on the first pitch. He clips a foul with a swing so mighty that the follow-through staggers him across the plate to the other side.

Astudillo steps back, taps his spikes with his bat, and settles into the batter's box. He lines the next pitch sharply but foul of the left-field pole. Fittingly, a man in one of the black Tortuga T-shirts comes up with the ball and holds it high for everyone to see.

Down 0–2 in the count, Astudillo checks his swing on the next pitch, which is outside. The catcher appeals to the first-base ump.

In the press box, a reporter says, "You can't call him out on La Tortuga Night."

He doesn't. The ump signals no swing. The fans exhale.

The next pitch is a breaking ball tailing off the far side of the plate. Astudillo swings—and connects, rapping a sharp grounder up the middle past the Orioles' diving shortstop. The Tortugans let out a roar and rise to their feet.

On the railing of the Twins dugout, Cruz and Rosario burst into a big laugh. They clap above their heads for Señor Barriga to see.

Morneau marvels that Astudillo was able to get the barrel of his bat on a ball so far off the plate. "That's what makes him special," he tells the home audience.

Giggles spread through the press box. It's as though the game's followed an improbable yet predictable script. Astudillo has played his part, stoking the legend.

The crowd chants, "La Tortuga! La Tortuga!"

Everyone's caught up in the moment. Morneau remarks, "That's pretty cool to see. For a guy who's grinded his way through the minor leagues, to get an opportunity and see everyone embrace him like that. It has to put a smile on your face."

Tomorrow afternoon, La Tortuga will start in right field. He'll lead off the seventh inning with a single and later make his way to third on a throwing error. He will tag up on Kepler's sacrifice fly to left and break for home. His face will strain with the effort but then, five strides from the plate, it will flash with pain, and when you look at the replay, you'll notice him pulling up on his left leg. His run will break a scoreless tie and put the Twins up 1–0 in a game they will eventually win 9–2. But Astudillo's expression will be serious as he makes his way through the congratulations in the dugout. He will spend the balance of the game on the bench, and the next day the Twins will place him on the 10-day injured list with a "left hamstring strain."

But for that moment, standing on first base Friday night, the ovation consummates "An Evening with La Tortuga." Astudillo feels the love cascading down from the stands and emitting from his teammates. Words can't quite capture this feeling, but he tries in an Instagram post the next morning along with a clip of his pinch hit: "Seriously, you all have no idea how much it means to me, someone who had to fight to get here, to hear this. Thank you. Sincerely, thank you."

Postscript

After coming back from his hamstring strain, Astudillo injured his oblique making a leaping catch in late June and missed much of the rest of the season, appearing in only 58 games with the Twins. He still managed to play every position except shortstop and pitcher and finished with more doubles (nine) than strikeouts (eight). At the start of the 2020 season, Astudillo was quarantined after testing positive for COVID-19 and saw limited action once cleared to play, appearing in only eight games during the shortened season, going 4-for-16 with no walks.

HANK GREENBERG: SUPERSTAR AND SCAPEGOAT

The Hebrew Hammer had a complicated relationship with the people of Detroit.

MICHIGAN HISTORY, SEPTEMBER/OCTOBER 2014

Introduction

Hank Greenberg grew up in the Bronx, played his last year of professional baseball in Pittsburgh, owned and managed teams in Cleveland and Chicago, and lived out his life in Los Angeles. But he is most identified with

Detroit, where he played for the Tigers from 1933 to 1946. You would think the city would have embraced the two-time MVP who led them to four World Series. But it wasn't that simple for a Jewish ballplayer there in the 1930s.

* * *

In the 1930s, a culture of anti-Semitism permeated the city of Detroit. Henry Ford, the paterfamilias of the Motor City, had published accusations purporting a Jewish conspiracy to subvert Christianity. Meanwhile, Father Charlies Coughlin, a priest at a suburban Catholic church, preached against "Jewish conspirators" and "moneychangers" to 10 million rapt listeners nationwide on his weekly radio show. Jews were a marked minority in Detroit, numbering only 75,000 among its almost 1.6 million residents. Country clubs excluded them. Hospitals wouldn't hire them. And many corporations had glass ceilings that kept Jews from rising to executive positions.

This was the environment the young Jewish baseball player Hank Greenberg encountered. In his first full year in the majors (1933), Greenberg endured anti-Semitic slurs not only from opponents, but from the hometown fans at Navin Field. The barbs burrowed under his skin. "The remarks about my Jewish faith made life for me a living hell," he writes in his autobiography *Hank Greenberg: The Story of My Life.*

On the other hand, he found support in his own community. He regularly dined in Jewish homes. He was invited to join the area's two Jewish country clubs: Franklin Hills and Knollwood. He also associated himself with the Young Men's Hebrew Association and the B'nai B'rith, a Jewish service organization.

Despite the challenges he faced, Greenberg finished 1933—his rookie year—with a solid .301 batting average and 12 home runs. He established himself as the team's regular first baseman and showed promise of developing into a key contributor for the Tigers.

Into the final month of the 1934 season, with Greenberg having a breakout year, he had won over not only the Jews of Detroit but the general population as well. The Depression had hit the Motor City hard. A mood of despair permeated the streets. Except at Navin Field, where the Tigers provided a diversion and elixir to misery. Leading the league, the Tigers imbued Detroiters with sense of civic pride.

Then the High Holy Days came around. Greenberg had promised his parents he would not play on Rosh Hashanah and Yom Kippur. But he also felt obligated to his teammates, especially since he had been carrying the team in those early days of September. Detroiters unsympathetic to his religious heritage—the Gentile majority—muttered, "Rosh Hashanah happens every year but we haven't won a pennant in 25 years."

He struck a compromise by attending synagogue the morning of Rosh Hashanah and playing that afternoon. During the game, he hit two home runs, giving the Tigers a 2–1 victory and inspiring local reporters to gush with praise for his contribution to the civic cause. In prose that reflected widespread sentiment, John M. Carlisle wrote in the *Detroit News*: "Henry Greenberg is something more off the playing field than a first baseman who has been one of the sparkplugs in the Tiger drive for a pennant. He is a finely bred young man with a high sense of duty."

Ten days later, when he sat out the game on Yom Kippur, the Tigers had already nearly clinched the pennant and Greenberg had won the fans' respect. Edgar Guest's poem "Speaking of Greenberg," published in the *Detroit Free Press*, reflected the city's mood, giving Greenberg its blessing for honoring his heritage.

Even so, when the Tigers lost the World Series, some grumbled that Greenberg had failed to come through in the clutch. He would learn that the people's embrace depended on his ability to satisfy their expectations.

The following year, Greenberg had another outstanding season, winning the Most Valuable Player (MVP) Award and leading the Tigers back to the World Series. He broke his wrist in the second game of the Series, and was willing to play in Game Six on Yom Kippur to help the team. However, the pain prevented him from being able to grip a bat or catch a ball. The Tigers managed to win without him.

Also in 1935, team owner Frank Navin died, leaving Walter O. Briggs Sr. to take over. Soon after, a fissure opened between management and Greenberg. Figuring he deserved a handsome raise after his MVP year, the first baseman held out for more money than Briggs was willing to pay. That established him as a divisive figure. Some fans took his side during the negotiations, but the majority was not sympathetic to a ballplayer demanding more money when the Depression had cut the average worker's wages. The press dubbed him "High Henry" for seeming to place himself above others.

Greenberg and Briggs finally came to terms, and Greenberg got off to a hot start in 1936. But 12 games into the season, he reinjured his wrist and had to sit out the rest of the year. Greenberg came back the following season to drive in 183 runs, one shy of breaking the American League single-season record (Greenberg's 1937 total was later adjusted to 184, though Lou Gehrig's single season record set in 1931 was also adjusted by one run, up to 185). And in 1938 he electrified the city with his pursuit of Babe Ruth's single-season home run record. He fell two short, finishing with 58, but his attempt had entertained and pleased Tiger fans.

Greenberg had another good season in 1939, making the All-Star team for the third year in a row, but his remarkable play the two previous seasons had raised expectations. The fans got on him when he didn't perform at his previous level. He felt they had turned on him. Amid rumors that the Tigers planned to trade him to the Yankees, Greenberg complained to *New York World-Telegram* writer Dan Daniel: "No human being can take that sort of thing daily—and overcome it. Maybe I am too sensitive. But that's the way I am constituted, and that's the way baseball and the fans in Detroit will have to take me. They can't say that I am not giving 100 percent of Greenberg to the Tigers on and off the field."

The Tigers didn't trade Greenberg, but the Detroit press and fans jumped on him for his printed comments. The *Detroit News* ran an editorial with the heading "Sensitive Hank," in which it sarcastically asked fans to let up because the ballplayer couldn't take it. Still mired in the Depression, the people of Detroit expressed little sympathy for the woes of someone they saw living a privileged life. At the same time, the *Detroit Jewish Chronicle* speculated that anti-Semitism was the root cause of the boos and criticism directed Greenberg's way.

In 1940, Greenberg repaired his reputation when he moved to left field to make room for hard-slugging but poor-fielding Rudy York on first base. The Tigers won the pennant that year, and Greenberg earned his second MVP Award. The local and national press praised him for his selfless, team-first attitude in agreeing to the position switch. But when the *Free Press* printed complaints by Greenberg—taken from a conversation with sports editor Charles Ward that Greenberg had thought was off the record—about Tiger management forcing him off first base, the story disillusioned many fans.

Then came the draft. In early 1941, before the United States had entered the war, Greenberg requested in the confidential questionnaire he returned to the draft board that he be deemed Class 2, or irreplaceable at his position—an accurate assessment regarding his place on the Tigers, but one commonly reserved for people in vital industries, such as aircraft or armament plants. Before America had entered the war, he wanted to be able to make what he could playing ball. When a draft board member leaked Greenberg's request, it polarized public opinion among the Detroit working class. It also touched off a national debate on the right to pursue personal wealth in a capitalist society versus one's duty to a citizen army. Once again, Greenberg situated himself at the heart of controversy.

His position provoked bigots to write nasty letters sent to Greenberg in care of the Tigers. They included this missive: "Any bastard who says money first, my duty later, should be voted the most valuable player in Hitler's league and not the American League." And this one: "No wonder the world folks are more and more against the Jews race and you are [not] aiding to overthrow that opinion by being a slacker."

Greenberg hoped that Briggs would intervene on his behalf and have his induction deferred until after the 1941 season. But all Briggs did was instruct his management not to comment on the situation.

When the day of Greenberg's induction finally came in early May, less than a month into the 1941 season, he went willingly and became a model soldier stationed at Fort Custer. But that didn't stop him from asking Briggs to expedite his release from the army after Congress changed draft regulations to release men 30 years old and over from service. When the Tigers' owner declined to do so, Greenberg told a Washington, DC, reporter that he would never play for Detroit again. His anger dissipated a month later during the Armistice Day parade, perhaps softened by the reception he received from Detroit fans lining the street to applaud him. When Greenberg was honorably discharged on December 5, 1941, he declared his intention to return to the Tigers.

Two days later, the Japanese attacked Pearl Harbor, and Greenberg won a spot in the hearts of all Americans when he became the first major-league ballplayer to reenlist. He could have said he had already done his bit or waited for the call-up, but he willingly set aside his personal interest for the common good.

During the next three seasons, Greenberg served in the Army Air Forces in various roles in several U.S. locations and for eight months in China, where he was the administrative commanding officer of the 58th Bombardment Wing that began the B-29 bombing campaign of the Japanese homeland. He left the service in mid-June 1945, once again with plans to return to the Tigers.

A J. L. Hudson ad in the local papers addressing Greenberg summed up the civic mood in the postwar period: "All Detroit Is Rooting for You and the Tigers." They had plenty to cheer about in Greenberg's first game back on July 1, 1945, when he hit a home run, suggesting that it would be possible for the stars in active duty to return to their sport and restore the national pastime to its prewar glory.

He sustained that sentiment through the final day of the season, when he hit a grand slam in the ninth inning to clinch the pennant for the Tigers. Fifty years later, U.S. senator Carl Levin, who had listened to that game on the radio as a boy, recited the lead in the next day's newspaper: "'Call him the hero of heroes. Call him the champion of champions. Call him the hero of Bengaltown.' I almost weep remembering what it meant to us, that home run."

Greenberg took Tigers fans' joy to a new level when he led the team to victory in the World Series. But the following season proved difficult for the 35-year-old. He had married before the season, and his priorities were shifting. Baseball had become a job, one he played from memory. Back at first base, he did not perform to his prewar levels of prowess in the field or at the plate, and the fans expressed their impatience with boos—even when he missed a ball in warm-ups. Some of his teammates resented his $55,000 salary—highest in the majors. Frustrated, Greenberg wanted to quit. The son of the owner talked him out of it, but not before an irreparable rift developed with Briggs Sr.

Before the season, Greenberg had negotiated a contract for $75,000, and asked that $20,000 of that be deferred until he retired. Tigers general manager George Trautman told the first baseman that he wouldn't get that $20,000 if he quit—which was clearly stated in his contract. When Greenberg protested, Trautman consulted Briggs, who had the contract amended so Greenberg would receive the $20,000 if he retired before the season ended. Greenberg was not mollified, and Briggs was angered by his star's seeming lack of gratitude. Though Greenberg had a late surge to overtake Boston's Ted Williams and lead the league in home runs (44) and RBIs (127) that season, that didn't win him any friends in the front office. He had already sealed his fate with the Tigers.

On January 1, 1947—Greenberg's 36th birthday—*The Sporting News* ran an article with the headline "Hank Hints He'd Like to End Career as Yankee." The writer claimed he had the inside scoop, that Greenberg would "definitely" not play first for the Tigers, but would be "delighted" to do so for the Yankees. The writer got several facts wrong in his reporting. Greenberg would have liked to finish his career in the city where he grew up, but he had not initiated any defection from Detroit. The kicker was a photograph alongside the article that showed Greenberg holding up a Yankee uniform.

Two of the local dailies rebuked the first baseman. The *Detroit Times'* Bob Murphy led the attack: "He has insulted Detroit baseball fans by posing in the off-season with a Yankee uniform. That is proof enough for me Greenberg does not want to come back to Detroit as a player. I think the Tigers should respect his wishes." He spoke for some, but not all fans. Greenberg still had his admirers. But there were similar cries of disappointment over his perceived disloyalty.

Greenberg was understandably outraged. The photo had been taken three years earlier—when he had played in a War Bond game in New York—but the paper had passed it off as though it were current. Briggs made no attempt to investigate; the incident gave him the perfect opportunity to dump Greenberg and his inflated salary. The Tigers' owner promptly waived the star out of the league and into the hands of the Pittsburgh Pirates.

Briggs's action stunned and stung many Detroit fans. They had lost a hero. Art Neff was 11 years old on January 19, 1947, when he read the awful news in the Sunday newspaper. "I still remember the devastation I felt on that morning when I picked up the *Free Press* with the headline 'Greenberg Sold to Pirates,'" Neff said more than 60 years later. "The hurt was there for a long time."

Nobody was hurt more than Greenberg. He heard the news over the radio. No phone call from the front office. Just a telegram later from the general manager informing him that his contract had been assigned to Pittsburgh. Greenberg had played 1,292 games for the Tigers and given Detroit fans plenty to cheer. Only to be discarded like yesterday's trash. That wound ran deep.

Greenberg played his final season, 1947, for the Pirates. The following year, Cleveland Indians owner Bill Veeck invited Greenberg to join his team's front office. Greenberg stayed through 1956, running the team as general manager the last eight years. In 1959, he rejoined Veeck, this time with the Chicago White Sox as a co-owner. He also served as general manager for part of the 1961 season before resigning. Greenberg and his first wife, Caral Gimbel, had divorced in 1959. He married Mary Jo Tarola in 1966, and the couple moved to Beverly Hills in 1974, where Greenberg played tennis almost daily at the Beverly Hills Tennis Club. He was awarded an eternal place in Cooperstown in 1956 when the National Baseball Hall of Fame inducted him.

Throughout all those years and places, the way Detroit had released him hurt so much that Greenberg had returned to the city only a handful of times. So it was especially gratifying to Greenberg when the Tigers invited him back to Detroit for a special ceremony on June 12, 1983, to retire his number along with Charlie Gehringer's. On that day, between games of a doubleheader against the Indians, Greenberg, then 72, and Gehringer walked across the grass to the folding chairs set up for them in the infield. The Tigers gave the two men framed replicas of their uniforms, and Chrysler CEO Lee Iacocca donated new LeBaron convertibles to parade the legends around the field.

When Greenberg took his turn at the microphone, he told the 34,124 fans present, "Little did I dream that fifty-three years ago when I first played in Navin Field and popped up to Tony Lazzeri of the Yankees that I would come back here for such a day as this one."

He walked off the field that day with the best feeling Detroit had given him in a long, long time.

Postscript

These days, the citizens of Detroit seem to have forgotten any hard feelings for Greenberg. He's widely remembered as one of the team's biggest stars. Along the left-field wall of Comerica Park, he is immortalized in a statue, one of six alongside fellow Tiger greats Ty Cobb, Charlie Gehringer, Willie Horton, Al Kaline, and Hal Newhouser.

THE GREAT JOSH GIBSON

He was so good, the truth of his exploits may be greater than the legend.

MEMORIES & DREAMS, WINTER 2020

Introduction

For years I had heard the stories of Josh Gibson's exploits spoken with an awe reserved for the likes of Paul Bunyan and Hercules. I wanted to know if it was true: Could anyone really be that good?

Once upon a time in Pittsburgh, Josh Gibson clobbered a ball so mightily in the bottom of the ninth inning that it disappeared into the twilight. The next day, with his team in Washington for a home and home series, a ball tumbled from the sky before the game began. When the Washington outfielder caught it, the ump yelled to Gibson, "You're out! In Pittsburgh, yesterday!"

Or so goes the story. Gibson's talent was so large the only way to describe it accurately is through hyperbole.

There are reports of him hitting 84, even 90 home runs in a year. His plaque at the National Baseball Hall of Fame credits him with "almost 800" home runs. Bill Johnson, author of Gibson's biography for the Society for

American Baseball Research, claims, "He may have homered close to 900 times in various settings." Bill James believes the power-hitting catcher would have hit more than 500 if he'd been allowed to play in the major leagues (note that's at least 100 more than any other MLB catcher [Mike Piazza hit 396 at that position]).

Gibson's baseball-reference.com page lists only 113 home runs over 16 seasons with the Homestead Grays and Pittsburgh Crawfords. Yet elsewhere on the site, he is credited with 168 home runs during his time with those two teams. Add in 44 round-trippers during two seasons in the Mexican League, and that gives him 212 for his career. Research by the Special Committee on the Negro Leagues that examined Gibson's case for consideration of his induction into the Hall of Fame uncovered 224 career homers. Seamheads, which has compiled the definitive Negro Leagues statistics, credits Gibson with 238. The "official" totals seem hardly enough to earn comparisons as "the Black Babe Ruth."

But it's not about the numbers. Playing in the Negro Leagues throughout the 1930s and '40s, plus several more in Puerto Rico, Mexico, and the Dominican Republic, he impressed fans, teammates, and opponents with his talent. "There is a catcher that any big league club would like to buy for $200,000," Walter Johnson, the Washington Senators' great pitcher, said. "His name is Gibson. He can do everything. He hits the ball a mile. He catches so easy he might as well be in a rocking chair. Throws like a rifle. Too bad this Gibson is a colored fellow."

Alas, as a Black man who died only three months before Jackie Robinson integrated Major League Baseball, Gibson played at a time and in places where records were not neatly kept. We can't go back and scour the box scores or scorecards from each of his games to tally up an exact total of his home runs because they don't exist. But the truth of his talent is not to be found in the statistics; it's in the testimony of those like Johnson who saw him play.

Based on their reports, Bill James classifies Gibson as "probably the greatest catcher in baseball history" (sorry, Yogi and Bench) and "probably the greatest right-handed power hitter" (with all due respect to Messrs. Aaron and Mays). Drop the "probably" qualifier, and you could justify the argument in either case. Monte Irvin said his Negro Leagues contemporary Gibson had "an eye like Ted Williams and the power of Babe Ruth." Indians and White Sox owner Bill Veeck called Gibson the greatest hitter he ever saw. Dodger great Roy Campanella took it a step further, declaring that Gibson was "not only the greatest catcher but the greatest ballplayer I ever saw." Indeed, when they played together as teammates, it was Gibson behind the plate and Campy relegated to third. "Everything I could do, Josh could do better," Campanella said.

The Gibson legend began before his first professional game. Born December 21, 1911, in Buena Vista, Georgia, to a sharecropper who moved his family in 1926 to Pittsburgh where he became a steelworker, Gibson had grown to 6-foot-1 and 200 pounds by age 16. Tales of his power hitting with the semipro Crawford Colored Giants attracted the attention of the Homestead Grays' player-coach Judy Johnson. "I had never seen him play, but we had heard so much about him," Johnson said. "Every time you'd look at the paper you'd see where he hit a ball 400 feet, 500 feet." So perhaps it was not a surprise on July 25, 1930, when the Grays' catcher broke a finger in a night game (and the backup catcher was playing the outfield) that the Grays summoned the 18-year-old Gibson out of the stands to fill in—and he finished the season with the team.

A man of tremendous strength, Gibson swung a 41-ounce bat, heavier than most, which put an exclamation point on the balls he hit. Buck O'Neil, the Kansas City Monarchs legend, said there was a distinct sound of the ball coming off Gibson's bat that he had heard when only one other man made such contact, Babe Ruth. (Years later, O'Neil heard Bo Jackson make the same sound hitting a ball.)

Indeed, a little more than two months after his debut with the Grays, Gibson announced himself with a bomb during the playoffs that was the first ever to clear Forbes Field's 457-foot center-field fence. Two days later, on September 27, people like Judy Johnson and the Chicago American Giants' Jack Marshall insist they saw him hit a ball at Yankee Stadium that went over the roof. Not even Ruth managed such a feat.

Gibson didn't bloop fly balls over the outfield fence—he blasted them into history. He crushed one ball into the Polo Grounds' upper deck. He clobbered a 500-foot shot in Sportsman's Park. He nailed a 540-foot homer in Municipal Stadium. Launched a rocket over the roof of Shibe Park. And baked a tater in Puerto Rico estimated at 600 feet.

The distances were estimated by eyewitness accounts, which may have stretched them beyond their actual length. Had he hit those balls today and they'd fallen under the scrutiny of more precise estimates based on dozens of measurements paired with ball velocity and height data, the distances would no doubt come up shorter. But it wasn't the eye-popping numbers that impressed Gibson's contemporaries as much the enormity of his skills. They may have stretched the numbers to fit the feats.

Gibson obviously didn't hit the ball an actual mile—as Walter Johnson claimed—but he clouted it with such force that it seemed to travel that far.

"If someone had told me that Josh hit the ball a mile, I would have believed them," said Sam Jethroe, the center fielder whose Negro Leagues career overlapped Gibson's.

When Gibson came to the plate, others expected him to deliver—not simply a hit, but a bomb. Another story, probably apocryphal, underscores the point. One day in the Mexican League, Gibson had four hits, including a double and a triple. Afterward team owner Jorge Pasquel asked, "What's wrong?"

"What do you mean?" Gibson replied. "I went four-for-four."

"I got Willie Wells and Ray Dandridge for doubles and singles," Pasquel said. "I got you for home runs."

You can't pull up Gibson's home run highlights on YouTube or MLB.com—he played before even color television was invented—so we have to rely on testimony from those who saw him play in person. Like Satchel Paige, whose career spanned 30 years and thousands of batters. Paige said simply, "Josh was the greatest hitter I ever pitched to."

Or Irvin. "I played with Willie Mays and against Hank Aaron," Irvin said. "They were tremendous players but they were no Josh Gibson."

On January 1, 1943, Gibson had a seizure and passed out. He ended up in the hospital. The press reported he had suffered a nervous breakdown, but the true cause was eventually diagnosed as a brain tumor. Gibson had known early heartbreak. In August 1930, less than three weeks after his debut with the Grays, his wife died giving birth to the couple's twins. By the 1940s, his drinking and drug use had intensified. He endured frequent headaches and gained weight. Though he continued to hit consistently—averaging .368 from 1943 to 1946—and with power, clouting prodigious homers, his body gave out on him January 20, 1947.

Gibson died at age 36. Had he lived and stayed healthy, he no doubt would have played longer and hit more home runs to bolster his legend. Still, even though his career ended early, he hit more home runs—and with greater force—than perhaps any other man to play the game in North America. And that will be remembered long beyond the numbers.

Postscript

Major League Baseball announced in December 2020 it would incorporate Negro Leagues statistics into its official records, but that will not make Gibson—with his "almost 800" home runs—the new Home Run King, ahead of Barry Bonds, Hank Aaron, and Babe Ruth. No, Gibson's 238 homers will rank him 264th on the MLB all-time list, tied with Earl Averill, Ray Lankford, and J. D. Martinez (at the start of the 2021 season).

TONY O

Tony Oliva rose from humble Cuban roots to become a baseball legend.

ARTFUL LIVING, FALL 2015

Introduction

I was born in 1964, the year Tony Oliva was the American League Rookie of the Year and won the first of two consecutive batting titles. By the time I came of age as a fan, injuries had crippled his body, and it was too late for me to appreciate his full talent. Fortunately, the designated-hitter rule in 1973 extended his career, so I was at least able to see him play, if only as a shadow of himself. In my mind's eye, I can still picture him in the batter's box, his wounded knees sagging together. But there's a story to be told before those days, I discovered.

Maybe you've seen him pitching Wiffle balls to kids in a makeshift ballpark at the state fair or talking to current Twins behind the batting cage at Target Field or at Tony O's Cuban sandwich stand on the concourse. You may even have bumped into him around town at the car wash or post office or Dayton's. If you're lucky enough to be of a certain age, you saw him bat at Met Stadium, driving balls across the outfield with the powerful swing that tormented American League pitchers.

Over the past half century, Tony Oliva has become a fixture of the local community—one of its most recognizable and loved residents. The former eight-time All-Star's official title with the Twins these days is minor-league hitting instructor, but his larger, unofficial role is team ambassador. Sitting in the Twins clubhouse before a recent home game, Oliva, age 77, dressed in a blue TC windbreaker, white baseball pants, and black New Balance running shoes, reflects—in his strong, distinctive accent—on the unlikely path from his humble Cuban roots to his place as a Minnesota legend.

Born July 20, 1938, the third of 10 children and oldest son, Oliva grew up on a square-acre farm in the Pinar del Rio province, where his family raised cows, pigs, chickens, oranges, mangos, corn, and tobacco. He milked cows, planted crops, and developed a strong work ethic. The family of 12 lived in a three-bedroom house without electricity and plumbing. "It was crowded," he says. "But you get used to it."

His father, a former baseball player, carved a diamond into their land and introduced the island nation's favorite sport to his sons. They whittled bats from the branches of majagua trees. Sometimes their father returned from trips to Havana with gloves and balls. They had to make those balls last, though, and after the cover had worn off, they wrapped the balls with tape.

Tony's skills stood out. He could hit farther, throw harder, and run faster than the other boys. Soon he was playing regularly for the local town team. When others saw how good he was, they invited him to play for a better team in the bigger town of Entronque de Herradura, five miles away. That led to a spot on the Los Palacios nine, another jump up in the level of competition, when he was 17 years old.

The talented youngster wasn't thinking about playing major-league baseball in the United States. His dream was to play professional baseball in Havana for his favorite team, the Cienfuegos Camaroneros. He listened to their games on the radio and reveled in the exploits of pitchers Camilo Pascual and Pedro Ramos. Young Tony worked to improve his natural talents. "I dedicated myself to play more, to practice to be good," he said. "It's like school. If you don't study, you don't get smarter."

That paid off. His Los Palacios teammate, Roberto Tapanes, who had played minor-league baseball in the United States, recommended him to Joe Cambria, the Italian-born scout for the Washington Senators and Minnesota Twins who had signed more than 400 Cuban players to contracts.

Oliva impressed Cambria in a Havana tryout, and the Twins offered him a contract for $250 a month. That was more money than some families made in a year, which excited Tony, but he was not sure what his parents would think of their eldest son leaving the island. He knew another Cuban prospect whose parents had not let him leave. He asked Tapanes to broach the idea with his parents. Turned out they saw it as an excellent opportunity. "They were happy," Oliva says. "They said, 'We want the best for our son.'"

So in early April 1961 the 22-year-old left home, figuring he would return to Pinar del Río in the fall after the season ended. He and 21 other prospects got delayed for 11 days in Mexico waiting for their visas to enter the United States. By the time Oliva got to the Twins' rookie camp in Fernandina Beach, Florida, tryouts were almost over. In the four remaining intrasquad games, he hit well but struggled in the field. The Twins simply did not have room for all of the prospects, so they released him.

Oliva had come to the United States to play baseball. He did not want to return home and admit he had failed. Worse, the Bay of Pigs fiasco had occurred on April 17, further complicating relations between his home country and his host country, making it all but impossible for him to return to Cuba.

Cambria interceded on his behalf, and Oliva wound up with a rookie league club based in Wytheville, Virginia. There, he had to live in the colored section of town and walk three miles to and from the stadium. Segregation was an indignity he hadn't known in Cuba, where social status was determined more by money than skin color. He was embarrassed he did not know any English and afraid people would laugh at him if he tried. Someone wrote down "ham and eggs" and "fried chicken" for him, and for weeks that was what he ordered in the single restaurant in town that served Blacks until his vocabulary expanded.

He did better at the ballpark, batting .410—the best average in all of Organized Baseball—but he missed his family. The mail was lengthy and unreliable, so he communicated with them by occasional telegram, which cost $10–$15. Since there was no phone on the family farm, he would make arrangements to call them at a public telephone in town, but sometimes the lines for it were so long he was not able to make his call. Unlike today, when teams teach Latin prospects English and assign mentors to school them in American ways, Oliva and other Latin players during his day had to learn to survive on their own. "Those days, they threw you in there and you had to pick it up," he says.

After two more years in the Twins' minor-league system, Oliva earned a spot on the 1964 Twins. He felt intimidated the first time he walked into the Twins clubhouse and saw Harmon Killebrew, Bob Allison, Jimmie Hall, and Camilo Pascual—Pascual, whom he had heard play on the radio and now was seeing up close in person. "Coming from Cuba, coming from the country, and getting to the big leagues, I didn't know if I belonged," he says. "I was scared."

He quickly proved he did. In one of the most amazing debuts in MLB history, Oliva led the American League in runs scored, doubles, total bases, hits, and batting average (.323). He was selected as an All-Star and named Rookie of the Year. By the time he arrived for spring training in 1965, he knew he belonged, even when he started the season slowly. "I had so much confidence that I knew I was going to finish on top," he says. "I believed I can hit everybody and I can compete at this level."

He repeated as the American League batting champion, the first player in either league to start his career with two batting titles. He was an All-Star eight consecutive seasons and won another batting title in 1971 with a .337 average, the highest of his career. He quickly became a fan favorite.

Oliva benefited from the tutelage of his veteran Latin teammates, Pascual, Zoilo Versalles, and Vic Power, who were able to translate for him and teach him nuances of American culture, such as the importance of saying, "thank you" and "excuse me," phrases not used as routinely in his native land. "They taught me all of these little things," he says.

His success made him miss his family back home even more. "When you succeed at something, you like to be able to share that with your family and friends," he says. He leans back in his chair, the sadness of five decades earlier still visible in his face. "I wasn't able to do that."

Ten years after leaving Cuba, he finally saw his mother and younger sister Felicia in Mexico when he played winter ball there during the 1971–72 season. He was able to introduce them to his wife, Gordette, a South Dakota native he had married in 1968. (They met when she asked him for an autograph.) By then they had had the first two of their three children. The following winter, his father and Felicia traveled to Mexico and returned with him to the United States for five months. Those were joyful reunions.

Later in 1972, Oliva returned to Cuba for the first time in 11 years. He had left a young man and came back a seasoned baseball hero. More than 100 friends and family members gathered at the farm to greet him. "When I touched the ground, I felt like I was walking on the air," he says.

He returned in 1981 and five years later in 1986. The past couple of decades, he has been able to travel home more frequently and with greater ease. Though his salary in the days prior to free agency and during Calvin Griffith's notorious penny-pinching ownership topped out at $105,000 in 1972, Oliva sent money home whenever he could to help his family and over the years bought eight homes for his parents and siblings. "To be able to play ball and get $250 a month and be able to help my family?" He shakes his head. "That was a big deal."

Strained relations between the United States and Cuba worked against Oliva's brother Juan Carlos, who pitched 10 years for the Cuban national team. Oliva thinks his younger brother had the talent to pitch in the major leagues, but he never got the chance.

Knee injuries—torn cartilage and shredded ligaments—hampered Oliva throughout his career, and though the implementation of the designated-hitter rule in 1973 extended his playing days, he never batted over .300 in a full season after winning his third batting title. Still, when he retired after the 1976 season, Oliva had a .304 lifetime batting average.

Tony O. has reached the age when the question rises, Would he do it all over again? No, he says. If he knew he would not have been able to return to Cuba and see his family for so long, he never would have signed with the Twins. He would have stayed and fulfilled his dream to play for the Cuban national team. "I did not know anything different," he says. "I was happy. In those days, the best for me was right there."

Since he did leave, he is content with the way his life played out and grateful for all that baseball has given him. "I want to say 'thank you' to the fans for being so nice to me," he says. "I still hear from a lot of them. That's the best thing. That they will never forget you."

Postscript

In 2014, Oliva received 11 votes from the Golden Era Committee, one short of gaining entry into the National Baseball Hall of Fame. He'll get another shot when the Veterans Committee votes again in December 2021. The case for a plaque in Cooperstown rests on his Rookie of the Year honors, three Silver Sluggers, eight All-Star selections, and .304 lifetime batting average. But his injuries hurt his career numbers—220 home runs, 947 RBIs, 870 runs, 1,917 hits—which fall below Hall of Fame standards. The shame of it is that if he had stayed healthy and continued to perform at the level he had for the first eight years of his career for even another five years, not only would I have gotten to see his talent in full bloom, but he would already be a member.

THE SHINING OF MARK HAMBURGER

The St. Paul Saints' ace pitcher is not your typical professional athlete.

CITY PAGES, AUGUST 2016

Introduction

Four hours before first pitch on a Thursday afternoon inside the St. Paul Saints clubhouse, players, coaches, and the manager mill about. They all subscribe to an unwritten dress code: T-shirt, gym shorts, mandals, and socks. The players model compact muscles and short hair. They're walking clichés, nearly indistinguishable.

Until Mark Hamburger arrives. Tall, scrawny guy in a green flannel open over gray T-shirt, blue jeans, barefoot but for flip-flops. A backward Bakersfield Blaze cap stuffed over his long brown hair, scruffy beard, aviator sunglasses. He's carrying a longboard.

He sees me waiting for him, extends his hand: "Hey, how you doing?"

Spotting the empty plastic cup in my hand, he asks, "You want another water or a Coke?"

Hamburger is the first college or professional athlete I have interviewed in over 30 years to offer me something to drink. *This should be interesting*, I think. And it is.

Mark Hamburger, this summer's star pitcher for the St. Paul Saints, is like no other ballplayer I've met. He reminds me of two other iconoclastic pitchers, Jim Bouton and Bill Lee—smart, thinks for himself, unafraid to speak his mind. At 29, Hamburger's still finding his way, still writing his story.

And he's quite the author.

Here's a guy with a 90-plus-mph fastball who prefers yoga to lifting weights, Whole Foods to McDonald's, the Tao over *Sports Illustrated*, his '89 Oldsmobile station wagon over a new Audi. He's comfortable talking about the way a higher power works in his life, is not carrying a cell phone, and lugs a hard-shell blue Samsonite on road trips. Other than the fact he lives in his parents' basement, he's far from your typical millennial, let alone professional ballplayer.

The CliffsNotes on Hamburger's career read like this: Local junior college flunkout signed by the Minnesota Twins at an open tryout. Traded to the Rangers, rose quickly through the minors to join the team for its 2011 World Series run. Demoted to minors, twice busted for smoking weed, saddled with a 50-game suspension. Graduated from Hazelden and did a stint with the Saints in 2013. Resigned with the Twins, spent all of last summer at triple-A Rochester, but passed on the chance to pitch as a reliever in the majors because it wasn't what he wanted. Wound up back with his hometown team.

The full story is even better.

Hamburger perches on the back of the bench in the Saints dugout. A flotilla of white clouds sails across the blue ocean sky. The night before, Hamburger won his seventh game in seven decisions. He has already done an hour of Vinyasa yoga as part of his recovery regimen and is at ease.

"The defining moment, my biggest downfall, was those two failed drug tests within two months," he says. He looks me in the eye, his Confederate grays unblinking. "Everything caught up with me. It's exactly what I needed."

Hamburger does not litter his speech with "um," "like," and "you know." He speaks in complete sentences—sincere, smart, articulate.

He started smoking weed as a teen and kept smoking into the big leagues. But somewhere along the way it stopped providing relief and began causing problems. In Center City, he surrendered and started to put things right in his life. His left arm, his nonpitching arm, has become a metaphor for how he lives now.

He pushes up his sleeve to reveal a kaleidoscope of interlinked geometric shapes. Each represents a loved one: his older sister, his two grandfathers, three friends who passed away. The design is a work in progress. He plans to add his mom and dad along with his grandmothers. "This arm I created to honor friends and keep people in my memory," he says.

Hamburger points to the largest shape, which looks like a pattern drawn by a Spirograph. Hamburger explains the tat's significance. "Picture a diamond a foot long inside each one of us. . . . Each diamond has one thousand facets, yet each facet gets covered with dirt and tar. Every day I have something to clean, something new to rid myself of or something to polish."

He looks at me with an open, guileless face. "My intention is that I always have room to grow. It is the job of the soul to clean each facet until all of them shine brilliantly, reflecting the colors of the rainbow."

Can you imagine having a conversation like this with Joe Mauer?

Nobody aspires to peak with the Saints, who play in the American Association, one of the lowest rungs of minor-league baseball. Players see their time here as a foothold on their way to larger ambitions. For a lucky few that means the major leagues.

Yet here's Mark Hamburger, who's already spent time in the majors—where he appeared in eight innings over five games—and played at the minor's highest levels, pitching for the modest Saints.

"I'm surprised he's still here," says manager George Tsamis, briefly a major-league pitcher himself. "He deserves to be in Triple A, but I'm glad he's with us."

Of course he is. Hamburger's the team ace, with a record of 11–2. He's led the league in wins, complete games, innings pitched, and winning percentage. Hamburger has the speed—he throws in the low 90s—and the control—70 percent of his pitches have been for strikes—that major-league scouts value. The consensus seems to be that it's only a matter of time before he returns to "The Show." Yet for now, he's here because, well, he's just not like other ballplayers.

*   *   *

Steve Hamburger remembers the first time he played catch with his son. Mark was three. "He threw the ball to me, just a rocket, straight and right at me," Steve says. "I threw it back to him, and he did it again. Usually kids throwing for the first time are pretty dorky, but I could tell from those first two tosses that he was a natural."

Mark is the third of Steve and his wife Cheryl's three kids. He did everything full speed, even walking in his sleep. When there was a call home from the school, they knew it was a teacher complaining about Mark. He rebelled at school, church, everywhere.

He liked sports but was skinny and did not appear to be the next Dave Winfield. He played basketball, rugby, tennis, football, and, of course, baseball, though he didn't make the Mounds View High varsity team until his senior year. That fall, as a wide receiver, he caught 16 touchdown passes, a testament to his budding athleticism. He grew eight inches from the end of his junior year to graduation.

Pro scouts weren't exactly lighting up his phone, and his grades weren't going to get him into Vanderbilt University, so he wound up at Mesabi Range College. There, he shone on the mound (11–0, 0.65 ERA) but not in the classroom (he was academically ineligible to enroll a second year).

So in the summer of 2007, Hamburger and a buddy impulsively attended a Twins tryout at the Metrodome.

The Twins liked what they saw: a 6-foot-4 20-year-old who hit 93 mph on the radar gun six times in a row. Within days, he was pitching for their rookie team in the Gulf Coast League.

*   *   *

Hamburger hasn't cut his hair for more than a year, since he buzzed it close to his scalp for the Twins' spring training. Knowing he already had "an outrageous personality," he did not want his long hair to compound any misconceptions of him in the conservative organization.

He has let it grow since, more than 16 months, and it's taking on a personality of its own—long, light brown locks that would make Samson blush. At first glance, that wild mane could give the wrong impression.

Before I met Hamburger, Tsamis, the Saints manager, told me, "Don't let the hair fool you. He knows what he's doing."

He's right. Most ballplayers traveling through Fargo, Winnipeg, and Lincoln on the American Association circuit can tell you where to find the best burger, the cheapest pitcher of beer, the preferred strip club. When Hamburger hits a new town, he scouts out the co-op grocery, an organic restaurant, and a yoga studio, while riding his longboard.

At home, where he lives with his parents in Shoreview, he enjoys hanging out with them in the backyard overlooking a nature preserve, chilling with teammates after a game at the Ox Cart or Bulldog, playing Frisbee golf, and paddleboarding.

Those who know Hamburger use different terms to describe him: free spirit, goofball, hippie. They mean it in a good way.

His agent, Billy Martin Jr. (yes, the son of that Billy Martin), tells it like this: Once Hamburger showed up on his radar, he asked a friend, Rangers pitching coach Mike Maddux, what he thought of Hamburger. "He looked at me real seriously and said, 'That kid is messed up.' Uh-oh, I thought. What's wrong here? 'Yep, that kid is messed up in a really good way.'"

Among the Saints, everyone agrees Hamburger is a great teammate. He could be aloof and arrogant. After all, he's been to "The Show." He could lord that over his teammates, drop names like those of former teammates Josh Hamilton, Mike Napoli, and Michael Young. But it's not like that.

Hamburger's the guy singing and dancing in the clubhouse. He choreographs home run celebrations in the dugout. He works with younger players. "Guys love having him around," Saints pitching coach Kerry Ligtenberg says. "He's always trying to pick them up."

When the team left on a June road trip to Sioux City, Hamburger wasn't scheduled to pitch. The plan was for him to stay in St. Paul. Instead, he drove down to be with his teammates. They appreciated that.

When catcher Maxx Garrett joined the team a week into the season, the Washington State native didn't know anyone in town and didn't have a car. Hamburger became his chauffeur. He also gave him a powered longboard so he could get around on his own.

One night, when Hamburger drove Garrett home after a game, Garrett discovered he had forgotten his keys and locked himself out. Hamburger invited Garrett to stay at his house. "When I woke up, he had fixed eggs, oatmeal with blueberries, and orange juice," Garrett said. "It was like being at a B & B."

In August 2008, Hamburger's second summer with the Twins organization, pitching for Elizabethton in the Appalachian League, he was traded to the Texas Rangers for Eddie Guardado, who famously quipped, "What? I was traded for a hamburger?"

Hamburger climbed through the Rangers' minor-league ranks with stops in Clinton, Iowa; Hickory, North Carolina; Bakersfield, California; Frisco and Round Rock, Texas, until he made his major-league debut on August 31, 2011.

He has a poster of himself delivering a pitch in his red Rangers jersey but does not remember the details. He was too jacked on adrenaline. (He retired Tampa Bay one-two-three in a single inning of work.) Disappointed not to be put on the Rangers' playoff roster, Hamburger consoled himself in Colorado during the offseason smoking bales of marijuana.

The following summer, he was back in the minor leagues, pitching for the Rangers' triple-A team in Round Rock, but not very well. They released him in June. The San Diego Padres picked him up but released him in less than a month. Houston claimed him off waivers, and he finished the season with triple-A Oklahoma City.

When he failed his second drug test in February 2013, Houston promptly released him. Hazelden picked him up. Hamburger initially resisted rehab, but deep down, he knew he had a problem. So did his parents. Steve Hamburger could see how weed was controlling his son. "Every time he hopped in the car and drove down the street, I was a wreck, praying 'God, don't let anything happen to him.'"

The healing began at Hazelden. There, father and son had a long, meaningful conversation. "It was the first time in ten years that we had talked for more than ten minutes," Steve says. "There was something settled in his mind. I could tell he had accepted that he needed to change."

At the end of Mark's 30-day stay, the treatment staff recommended aftercare, noting that the majority of people who did not attend aftercare went back to using drugs. That bit of advice did not have the intended effect upon Hamburger. It simultaneously offended and inspired him.

"Did you just tell me if I don't give you more money I will fail?" he asked. "That gave me more incentive."

He signed with the Saints for the 2013 season, on a mission to stay clean and revive his career. Because the Saints play in a league independent of Major League Baseball, his 50-game suspension did not apply.

Despite a 6–8 record, Hamburger put up some respectable numbers, including a 3.26 earned-run average. He also demonstrated durability, setting a club record for most complete games in a season (five), tops in the league. His performance was good enough to impress the brass across the river. The Twins purchased his contract and assigned him to their double-A team in New Britain, Connecticut, to start the 2014 season. He pitched eight games after serving his suspension and was promoted to triple-A Rochester.

Hamburger spent the balance of the 2014 summer and the entire 2015 season in Rochester, only a phone call away from the major leagues. He could have returned to Rochester this year with a very good chance of being promoted to the parent club, but it would have been as a reliever. He wanted to be a starter.

So he parted ways with the Twins last November. He had a chance to sign with the Chicago Cubs, who gave him a tryout, and with the Miami Marlins, who wanted to sign him after he won the Saints' opening game this year. But Mark said, "No, thanks."

Not many guys would have the cojones to buck opportunity like that, but Hamburger is intent upon doing it his way this time, more as an act of personal integrity than outright defiance.

He does not want to simply fill a role with a team. He doesn't want to be shuffled around at the whim of an organization. He wants to be a starter, like his favorite pitcher of all time, Satchel Paige, the rubber-armed wonder renowned for his control and ability to pitch until tomorrow.

"Satch was a starter," Hamburger says. "Only starters can get a no-hitter or pitch a perfect game. When I think of pitching, I think of going nine innings. I think in terms of pitching complete games."

This is anathema to the current dogma limiting pitch counts, which has rendered complete games an oddity. Nowadays, pitchers rarely complete games (only six MLB pitchers completed four games last season), and throwing more than 110 pitches a game is considered Herculean. Not surprisingly, Hamburger does not subscribe to this philosophy. "I am completely against pitch counts," he says. "I should be able to throw 140 pitches if needed."

Through his first 12 starts, Hamburger has pitched four complete games and thrown 120 pitches or more in four outings.

While many pitchers spend hours lifting weights, believing bigger is better, Hamburger attributes his arm stamina to stretching and Vinyasa yoga, which he started practicing seriously post-Hazelden. He's lucky that he has never had a serious arm injury. "You can't break Gumby," he likes to say.

It's not that he sees himself as invincible. He's suffered enough to know that's not the case. It's just that he believes he can make it back to the big leagues on his terms.

They say abusing drugs stunts emotional growth, and that recovery allows addicts to resume growing up. Contrasting the Mark Hamburger of 2013, during his last stint with the Saints, with the Mark Hamburger of today provides a measure of newfound maturity. "He's done a lot of growing up," says Ligtenberg, the pitching coach. "Three years ago, he was not as polished. This year, he is locating his fastball inside and outside. He is taking it more seriously. He's prepared for his starts. He's not just throwing hard but has become more of a pitcher, picking his spots, changing speed."

The maturity has manifested itself in his personal life as well. Steve Hamburger says he and his wife enjoy having Mark at home now. "He's gotten a little bit of the beast out of him," Steve says. "I don't have to worry about him anymore."

The kid who his dad says used to move at 100 mph has learned to appreciate life in the slow lane. Mark prefers cooking food over a bonfire, washing clothes on an old-fashioned washboard, and queuing up LPs on a record player instead of listening to music through his phone. "I like the slower life," he says. "It creates a mindful practice."

He has been spending his downtime working with his brother Paul, a master welder and carpenter, on restoring a 1960 camper. He plans to move out of his parents' house at the end of the season and take up residency in the camper, breaking it in with a trip to the North Shore. "I'm going to practice tiny living," he says.

Mark's interactions with fans also show how he's matured. In Rochester, he sang the national anthem on Fan Appreciation Night, the Red Wings' final home game of the season. Afterward, the fans saluted him with a standing ovation.

Another night in Rochester, he signed autographs for 45 minutes while fans waited for the start of a postgame concert. "Nobody else does this," one Red Wings fan told him. "We really appreciate this."

At CHS Field, Hamburger catches the ceremonial pitches on nights when he's not scheduled to start, returning the ball with a hug to the honorary pitcher. He runs the errand of delivering a batting helmet to the kid sitting with the ball boy down the right-field line. But instead of trotting back to his teammates, he squats to chat with the kid for a few minutes. On his way back between innings, he pauses to greet fans he recognizes in the front row.

At the end of the game, when Saints players toss oversized stuffed balls into the stands, Hamburger points to a fan behind the protective screen above the dugout and throws the ball playfully toward him, knowing it will bounce back off the screen. He laughs then goes around the screen and flips the souvenir to the fan.

Maturity has also altered his ambition. When he was younger, big money was the draw. "The goal used to be about going to the big leagues and getting your pension," he says. No longer. "I've let go of that. Being a millionaire now has no allure."

If it were about the money, he could easily be earning more than his current $2,000-a-month salary pitching in Korea or Mexico, but he prefers playing close to home before family and friends. He ticks off other perks: "My chiropractor, my masseuse, a great facility, a front office who cares about us. They promote being silly."

It's all part of the evolution of Mark Hamburger.

*   *   *

Shortly after 7:00 P.M. on a Friday night, a perfect summer evening for baseball, Hamburger stands behind the mound, facing the flag in center field, about to go for his 10th straight victory. Flanked by two Little Leaguers, Hamburger sways a few times back and forth at the hips, takes two deep breaths, and stands still. One of the Little Leaguers turns to him and says, "You're going to have a perfect game."

After the first batter singles to right, the second batter singles to left, the third batter advances the lead runner with a long fly, and the fourth batter bloops a single, driving home Fargo-Moorhead's first run, Hamburger has thrown a dozen pitches to four batters and is down 1–0 with two runners on and only one out. *That kid was so off*, he thinks.

Privately, he had known it was going to be a tough night. He has an open cut on the inside of his right index finger—right where he grips his split-finger fastball, his best pitch. "It was a test," he would say afterward.

He passed.

He induces the next batter to ground into a double play. Once his team has evened the score, he starts the second by striking out the first two batters on seven pitches and retires the third on a fly to left field.

When Hamburger jogs out to the mound to start an inning, his hair flapping up and down, he sometimes steps on the chalked first-base line. Many ballplayers consider that bad luck and hop exaggeratedly over the chalk, but Hamburger professes not to have any superstitions.

"Absolutely none," he says. Save one. On days he pitches, he brings a two-sided baseball card with him to the ballpark, with a picture of Satchel

Paige on one side and Sister Rosalind, the nun who gives Saints fans massages, on the other. It's stashed in his locker at the moment.

He watches his team's at-bats from the top step of the dugout, his hat off, his arms draped over the railing. When a line drive to left with the bases loaded scores two runs, he skips happily over to the dugout entrance to congratulate the two teammates who've just scored. After his catcher Tony Caldwell hits a two-run homer, Hamburger dances over to the entrance and organizes his teammates to form a canopy by standing opposite one another and clasping hands for Caldwell to pass under. Four innings later, he choreographs a slow-motion run from the opposite end of the dugout to celebrate Willie Argo's two-run homer that stretches his lead to 10–3.

On the mound, Hamburger works quickly and efficiently. He finishes his delivery with his chest tucked toward the ground and his right leg poking into the sky.

But he seems distracted by his cap. He takes it off several times and studies it, as though he's wondering whether he has accidentally grabbed a teammate's cap that doesn't fit quite right.

(I ask him about this after the game. "Wait a minute, let me see if he's still there," he says and ducks back to his locker. He returns with his hat and shows me a green beetle clinging to the back. "I thought he might have fallen off after I threw a fastball, but he was still there. I had to keep checking. . . . I named him Sammy Sosa, but after that guy homered, I figured that wasn't working so I renamed him Randy." After Randy Johnson, the Hall of Fame pitcher whom he idolized growing up.)

That settles his luck. The beetle hung on for the ride through the eighth inning.

That's when it stops looking easy for Hamburger. He gives up a home run then hits a batter with a wild pitch. (When the batter jogs to first, Hamburger apologizes.)

The next batter fouls off three pitches before Hamburger finally gets him to miss, which ends his night. He's thrown 120 pitches, 85 for strikes, fanned eight batters, walked none, and consistently fired his fastball in the low 90s.

He leaves with the score 10–4, which is how it stays to record his 10th consecutive win.

Afterward, the lack of media in the clubhouse reminds Hamburger of the humble level of his success. Only one reporter (yours truly) and two college students enrolled in a sports journalism internship ask to talk to him.

He graciously asks the students their names and shakes their hands. He patiently answers their questions. But he deflects mine about the injury to his cut finger with a laugh. Won't tell me how it happened. Which means there must be a good story there, hinting that I've only scratched the surface with him.

In the dugout on the first day we met, Hamburger smiled when I asked him about being able to pitch again in the major leagues. He likes the idea of it but is just not sure how or if it will happen. "The dream is evolving as I go," he says. "Nine years ago, the dream was about getting to the majors. The goal now is to be present. Last time I was here, I was picking up the pieces. Now I'm whole."

That's huge for him, the chance to play whole in his hometown for a first-place team that sells out night after night. Never mind that the stadium fills with 7,410 instead of 45,000 fans. Playing for the Saints is in keeping with his preference for the slower life. "The competition level is different, sure, but we play awesome baseball here before packed crowds," he says. "I'd like to consider this a big-league experience—without the private jet."

Postscript

Hamburger played the following summer with the Saints, with his 2017 numbers similar to the previous season: 13–6, seven complete games, 3.56 ERA, and 115 strikeouts in 172 innings. He played two seasons of winter ball in Australia during those years. On March 23, 2018, the Saints traded Hamburger to the New Britain (Connecticut) Bees of the Atlantic League (not the New Britain Rock Cats, the Twins' double-A affiliate for whom Hamburger played in 2014), where he went 10–8 with a 4.39 ERA and no complete games. That was his last season in professional baseball.

THEY CALL HIM KILLER

A conversation with Harmon Killebrew, one of the game's greatest hitters and nicest guys.

108 MAGAZINE, SPRING 2007

Introduction

With Harmon Killebrew chasing his 500th home run in the summer of 1971, my dad scored tickets to a game at Met Stadium. But only two tickets.

He had four children. Much to my dismay, my older sister won the ticket sweepstakes, so my father took her to the game. I had to stay home and listen on the radio. Exactly 35 years later to the day, on August 10, 2006, I was able to have a long conversation with Killebrew, which almost made up for not being able to witness his historic home run. He spoke to me by phone from his home in Scottsdale, Arizona.

During 22 seasons with the Washington Senators, Minnesota Twins, and Kansas City Royals (1955–1975), Harmon Killebrew hit 573 career home runs, surpassed only by Babe Ruth among American League sluggers. He hit 40 or more homers in a season eight times, drove in 100 or more runs nine times, played in 13 All-Star Games, and was named the American League MVP in 1969, when he led the league in home runs, RBIs, walks, and on-base percentage. His 393 home runs from 1960 through 1969 were more than any other big-league player hit that decade. Killebrew was inducted into the National Baseball Hall of Fame in 1984.

> JR: The night that you hit your 500th home run, my father had two tickets, but instead of asking me or my brother, he asked my older sister to go. I've never forgiven him for that.
>
> HK (laughs): That's too bad, doggonit.
>
> JR: It actually provided a very sweet moment for my sister and my dad. We could start there. What do you remember about that night and about hitting that monumental homer?
>
> HK: The interesting thing about my 500th home run was that the PR department, John Cassidy and Jack Breezy, had decided that they were going to do a commemorative cup and they picked a date that they were sure I would have hit my 500th home run. That day came, but I hadn't hit my 500th home run. They gave the cups away anyway. It seemed like it took about a month to hit that 500th home run, and when I did, it was against the Orioles. A curveball off Mike Cuellar. They stopped the game, and the people who had caught the ball, the whole family came down, and they gave me the ball. I gave them an autographed ball in return. When I came back into the dugout, [Twins manager] Bill Rigney said, "I hope it's not as long between 500 and 501 as it was between 499 and 500." I hit my 501st the next at-bat.
>
> JR: So you showed him!
>
> HK: Well, it was kind of a mental thing more than anything else, I think, because 500 didn't break a record or anything, but it was a significant number.

JR: You had so many accomplishments over your career. And then you finished second only to Babe Ruth in total homers for the American League.

HK: That record still stands and it's number one right-handed home run hitter at the present time.

JR: What are you most proud of as an accomplishment in your career?

HK: I suppose I'll always be remembered for hitting home runs, so I would say for being the number one right-handed, home run hitter in American League history all these years. It looks like that's going to change in the upcoming years with guys like Alex Rodriguez. [It did. Rodriguez retired with 673 home runs, bumping Killebrew to number three all-time. Rodriguez, who batted right, also edged ahead of Killebrew for top place as the right-handed hitter with the most home runs all-time in the American League.]

JR: How about your biggest disappointment? When you think about your career, is there anything you wish you had been able to do?

HK: I think '67 was one of the biggest disappointments, because we went into Fenway Park with a one-game lead and two games to play. We were leading that first game. Jim Kaat pitched against the Red Sox that day, but he hurt his elbow and had to be taken out of the game. We ended up losing the game. We went into the final day of the season tied with the Red Sox. Dean Chance pitched that one, and we ended up losing it. That was a really big disappointment. The Red Sox went to the World Series and played the Cardinals and lost to them, and we went home to Minnesota.

JR: Didn't you bat in the bottom of the ninth in the seventh game in 1965?

HK: I got the last hit off Koufax in that World Series.

JR: I remember reading an account of that game, and I saw the lineup. It was Oliva, you, and Earl Battey. I knew how the game turned out. I knew the Dodgers won, but I thought, "Boy, with this lineup, maybe somehow they'll do it."

HK: I got that hit off Koufax, and I was on first base and then Battey and Bob Allison made outs. Bob was the final out. He struck out to end the game and then took his bat and hit the ground. I told him after the game, if he'd have swung as hard at the ball as he swung at the ground, we might have won the game.

JR: How did he respond?

HK: Bob and I were good friends, so he knew I was kidding him.

JR: Good. He didn't take a swing at you?

HK: No, no.

JR: Can you tell me the story of how Washington Senators scout Ossie Bluege discovered you playing in a pickup game in your hometown of Payette, Idaho?

HK: I had graduated from high school. I was playing semipro baseball at the time. I don't know if you'd even call it semipro, nobody got paid anything. I talked to scouts from every ballclub except Washington and one other I can't remember. I had accepted a scholarship to play baseball and football at the University of Oregon. I really hadn't planned to sign at that time, but we had a United States senator from Payette by the name of Herman Welker. He kept telling [Senators owner] Mr. Griffith about a kid in Idaho that he thought could help him win some games. In those days, they weren't winning many games. They were always "first in war, first in peace, and last in the American League." Anyway, I think more than anything else, just to keep Senator Welker quiet, Mr. Griffith sent Ossie Bluege out to see me. He had rented a car in Boise, about sixty miles from Payette, and drove over. I was sitting in the car with him. It was a rainy day and didn't look like we were going to play the game. He said the Washington Senators wanted me to come to Washington to work out with the ballclub and I told him I appreciated that, but I was going to go to the University of Oregon and play football and baseball. As it turned out, the skies cleared. People knew that there was a major-league scout there, and they actually burned gasoline on the infield to dry it up. I guess they wouldn't do that today with the price of gas. (laughs)

I had never seen anyone hit one over the left-field fence in that park. I heard that way back in the '30s or '40s someone had done it. That night I hit one over that fence. Mr. Bluege went out the next day and stepped it off. It landed in a bean field—some people said it was a potato field, but it was a bean field—and said it was 435 feet. He thought that was a pretty good hit for a seventeen-year-old kid, so he called Mr. Griffith and said, "Maybe we should try to sign this kid."

As it turned out, in those days they had a bonus rule that if you signed anything over the minimum salary, which was $6,000, you were considered a bonus player and had to stay with the big-league club for two years. Well, it ended up I signed that contract and went directly to the major leagues and stayed there for two years, before they could send me to the minor leagues.

JR: Right, and then it took about five years when you were on the bench there instead of in the minors.

HK: Yeah, that was in 1954, and it took until 1959 before I actually became a regular player. But I thought if I went to college for four years and then had to go in the military for a couple of years—everybody was having to do that—then sign and go to the minor leagues for four or five years, by the time I got to the major leagues I'd be twenty-nine years old before I even got another opportunity.

JR: You were an All-American quarterback in high school and had a scholarship to play football at the University of Oregon. During that time, did you think, "Gosh, I wish I would have taken that scholarship and been playing football in Oregon"?

HK: Four years later [in 1958], the Oregon Ducks went to the Rose Bowl, and I always wondered if I'd have been there, would they have gone to the Rose Bowl? You know, you can play that "What if?" game all day.

JR: Can you tell me the story of your first home run when you were eighteen years old?

HK: That was against the Detroit Tigers in Griffith Stadium in 1955. Billy Camden was the veteran pitcher on the mound, and Frank House was the catcher. When I stepped into the batter's box, House said, "Kid, we're gonna throw you a fastball." I didn't know if he was telling me the truth or not. Sure enough there came a fastball, and I hit it 476 feet. I came around the bases, touched home plate, and he said "Kid, that's the last time we're ever going to tell you what's coming." And it was. Nobody ever said anything after that.

JR: Are there other home runs or big hits that stand out from your career?

HK: Oh, a lot of them. The first one, the last one, and a lot of them in between. Number one that I'll always remember is the one that I hit against the Yankees just before the All-Star break in 1965. That was in the bottom of the ninth with two outs. I kept fouling off pitches before I hit a 3–2 pitch off Pete Mickelson. They call it a "walk-off home run" now. That put us up by four games over the Yankees going into the All-Star break. They never caught us. We ended up winning the pennant that year.

JR: By the end of 1967, you were thirty-one years old, you'd hit 380 home runs, which is more than Babe Ruth had hit at the same age, but then you pulled your hamstring in the '68 All-Star Game.

HK: It was more than just that pulled hamstring. It was a really severe injury. I tore something below the knee, I tore some fascia, the covering of the muscle there, and then pulled a piece of bone away from the pelvis where the hamstring attached. A lot of doctors thought I was through playing. I worked hard over the winter, came back, and had the best year I ever had the next year. But it almost ended my career, that leg.

JR: Do you think you could have reached Ruth's mark of 714 if you had stayed healthy?

HK: That's a good question. I'll never know. That year I missed a whole half a season. I was leading the league in home runs and RBIs at the time. The same thing happened in 1965, the year we won the pennant. On August second, I dislocated my elbow on a play at first base and was out until the last ten games. I played third base those games and in the World Series.

JR: In '61, when the Senators were contemplating the move to Minnesota, the press reported that you weren't happy because you were worried that wind and cold might hurt the team's hitting. Was that true?

HK: I was disappointed but that wasn't the entire story. I was not overly excited about moving to Minnesota because I played in the American Association for a month in 1958 and one of the places I went to was the Twin Cities. I played in St. Paul and Minneapolis, against those two clubs, so I knew the weather wasn't going to be great. I liked playing with Washington because the weather was better, and the other thing was that we were just starting to become a good ballclub. We made a trade with the White Sox, we got Earl Battey and Don Mincher from them in exchange for Roy Sievers. We were developing players like Tony Oliva, Jim Kaat, and it just looked like we were going to become a good ballclub. I felt the fans in Washington deserved to see a winning club there.

JR: In retrospect, are you glad the team made the move?

HK: The rest of that story is that I really loved the fourteen years I played in the Twin Cities. The weather was still bad some of the time, but the people were wonderful there, my kind of people.

JR: Calvin Griffith said of you that "he was the meal ticket for our franchise for all those years in Washington and Minnesota." Yet toward the end of your career, your relationship with Calvin soured and you finished your career in Kansas City. What happened?

HK: At the end of my career, Calvin thought that I was through playing, but I thought I could play a couple more years. He said, "I'd like you to go manage our triple-A club near Tacoma, but you're welcome to talk to anybody you want to." I talked to a lot of different clubs. I ended up settling with Kansas City because I thought it fit my personality the best. They had a ballclub that was just coming along and I thought they had a chance to win. I went down there and the artificial turf was really tough on my knees. I ended up having to quit after that. I went down there with the idea that I was going to be their designated hitter all year, but it didn't work out that way. Jack McKeon was the manager. He had Tony Solaita, a left-handed hitter, hit against right-handers, and I hit against left-handers. Together, we had a pretty good year. We hit thirty home runs together. I hit fourteen and he hit sixteen.

JR: Back in Minnesota, on June 3, 1967, you blasted a home run to the second deck in left field, which was the longest ball ever hit in Met Stadium. It traveled an estimated 520 feet and smashed two seats—

HK: It was 800, John.

JR: Eight hundred feet? It gets longer over the years, doesn't it?

HK: I tell people the older I get, the farther that ball goes.

JR: No matter how far it was, the Twins painted those seats orange and never sold them. Were you embarrassed by that gaudy show of adoration they showed?

HK: Up in Washington, in RFK Stadium, Frank Howard had all the seats almost all white up there where he hit home runs, so I think it was kind of neat that they put that up there.

JR: One of those seats is bolted to the wall in the Mall of America amusement park [built on the site of the former Met Stadium]. Do you ever go to look at it or do you find it tacky?

HK: You've got to know where to look, but I've showed people that seat many times.

JR: You don't find it sacrilegious to step foot in the mall?

HK: No, I don't at all.

JR: You hold the Twins records for all-time home runs, RBIs in a season, as well as career home runs, RBIs, total bases, walks, strikeouts. Do you think anyone on the team today has a chance to surpass those marks?

HK: Oh, sure. If they play long enough. [So far, no one has.]

JR: You recently turned seventy, Happy birthday! How did you celebrate?

HK: My wife had a birthday party for me, and we had almost all of our family there. It was very nice.

JR: You didn't do anything crazy, like jump out of an airplane like President Bush did for his eightieth?

HK: No, no. I had a raft trip, though, did some whitewater rafting that day down the Clark River in Montana.

JR: Wikipedia quotes you as saying in response to the question "What do you like to do for fun?" It says, "I like to wash dishes." How would you amend that entry if you had a chance?

HK: That was a joke. Whoever wrote that took it as a serious thing.

JR: So what did you do for fun when you were a player?

HK: I used to fish and hunt a lot with my brothers over the years.

JR: And you've said, "Let's help those out who are in a greater need." How have you tried to do that?

HK: Over the years I've initiated several charity golf tournaments, one that I helped start in Sun Valley, Idaho, the Danny Thompson Memorial, is still going on. This will be the thirtieth year.

JR: I remember him, the Twins shortstop who died of leukemia. If we could talk about your bats for a minute. What size bat did you use as a player?

HK: Thirty-five inches and about thirty-three ounces.

JR: Did you change the weight during the course of the year?

HK: Just a little bit, maybe dropped down an ounce or so. Most of the guys, like Williams and Mantle, used about the same size bat.

JR: And who made your bats?

HK: I used a Louisville Slugger exclusively, all those years.

JR: Were you like Williams, going to the factory and telling them exactly how to hone them down?

HK: Yes, I did. And what kind of wood I wanted. Rex Bradley, there at the factory, would always pick out the type of wood that I wanted.

JR: You played first, second, third, outfielder in your career, often a couple of those in one game. Were you ever tempted to play all nine in the same game like your teammate Cesar Tovar did in '68?

HK: I could have, but no. I wasn't interested in doing that.

JR: Common folklore suggests that the silhouette of a player swinging a bat in the Major League Baseball logo is you. MLB denies that. What do you think?

HK: I don't know if they've denied it. They just haven't said that it's me.

JR: Do you think it is?

HK: I know it is.

JR: How do you know?

HK: I happened to be in the commissioner's office and saw the mockup of the picture they were using.

JR: In 1962 you won the RBI title while batting just .243, which is the lowest ever for any RBI champion. Did you take some grief for that from teammates and opponents?

HK: Well, that's a pretty neat trick, isn't it?

JR: It sure is.

HK: As a kid, I was a high average hitter. I hit the ball all over the park. One day in spring training when I was very young, Ralph Kiner, who was a great home run hitter in the National League for years, came up to me and said it looked like I was going to have some power. He said, "You're not going to be able to hit home runs consistently unless you pull the ball. Try moving up on the plate a little bit." I tried that, and it worked out pretty well. The thing is it leads to more strikeouts and also for a lower batting average.

JR: It seems a worthwhile trade-off to get more power. How do you think you would do against today's pitchers, if you were in your prime?

HK: If I was in my prime? I think all right.

JR: Do you see pitching as about equal to your day?

HK: Pitching is a lot thinner today than it was when I played.

JR: Because of expansion?

HK: That's one of the reasons. That's not to say that there aren't some great pitchers out there today, because there are. I think each club had more good pitchers in those days than they do today.

JR: Whom did you dread facing on the mound?

HK: Nobody. There were a few I couldn't hit very well, though.

JR: Who had your number when you'd come up?

HK: Stu Miller. He was a relief pitcher with Baltimore for five years and I couldn't hit the guy.

JR: Who did you especially like going up against and seem to do well against?

HK: One guy I had pretty good luck with was Rollie Fingers, and I don't know why, because he was a great pitcher. Seemed like the harder he tried to get me out, the better I hit him.

JR: What superstitions did you practice while playing?

HK: I didn't have any. Baseball, to me, is tough enough to play without having some superstitions that you've got to do in order to play the game. I asked Hank Greenberg one time what his superstition was. He said that after he hit a ball out of the ballpark, he liked to touch each base. I liked that one. That'll be mine.

JR (laughs): That's a good one. You've met seven presidents during your day. Which one strikes you as the most knowledgeable or avid baseball fan?

HK: Richard Nixon was really a very knowledgeable baseball fan. When I hit my 500th home run, he called me on the phone. We talked for about half an hour about baseball. I had met him when I was younger in Washington, and we talked baseball then. Ronald Reagan happened to be a great fan, too. You know, he did some broadcasting, and he was always full of the game. The two Bushes, both of them know baseball very well.

JR: Right, George W. can throw a strike, too.

HK: That's right. And another guy that was a pretty darn good athlete was Gerald Ford. I don't know if he was that knowledgeable about baseball, but I got to know him quite well.

JR: Football player from Michigan, and a golfer who, unfortunately, became famous for hitting fans in the galley with his shots. What do you think about guys who have passed you on the all-time home run list since you've retired, who are suspected of taking performance-enhancing substances?

HK: I don't think we've got all the information that we need to have in order to say exactly what those guys have done. I really don't want to make too big a comment about it. If they have, it's really disappointing to see players do that. The big issue is what's going to happen to their health five, ten, fifteen years down the road? And also, what kind of message are we sending to the youth of America?

JR: What did you see guys using during your day? Alcohol was obviously a drug of choice, but were amphetamines making it into the clubhouse?

HK: There were some in the game at that time. In fact I know that they were even offering those to the players, the trainers and the doctors were. They weren't illegal or anything. They did have seminars about them saying that they give you a false sense of being better than what you were, I guess. I know some of the guys that tried them told me all it did was keep them up all night. It really didn't do anything to enhance their ability to hit a baseball or play.

JR: There's a perception that back when you played it was a more innocent age. Would you agree with that?

HK: Oh, definitely. Not only baseball, but the country as a whole. It was a more innocent time I think.

JR: And was the game in any way more pure?

HK: I think we had a lot more fun playing the game than the guys do today. At least outwardly, they don't appear to be having as much fun as we did. It was a great time to play baseball. I think there were more great players in that era, in the '60s and early '70s, than any other era in the history of the game.

JR: You spent five years as a Twins broadcaster.

HK: A lot more than that!

JR: OK, how long was it?

HK: The first three years I did the Twins telecast. Then I did the Oakland A's for four years. I did the Angels for a year. Then I came back for several years and did the Twins telecast. I was there in '87 when they won the first world championship.

JR: Any favorite memories or highlights from that time?

HK: In 1987, I was doing the play-by-play when they actually clinched the pennant in Texas against the Rangers. That was a championship year, so that was a big deal for me. I was also at the game for the Twins in Anaheim when Rod Carew got his 3,000th hit, so that was a special thrill, because I saw him get his first hit in the major leagues and then to call his 3,000th hit, that was a special thrill for me.

JR: Well, it's certainly been a treat to talk to you. I appreciate your time.

HK: If you need to know anything else, call me again, John.

Postscript

Harmon Killebrew passed away from esophageal cancer on May 17, 2011, at the age of 74. I never had the occasion to call him back. He remains one of the nicest people I've been fortunate to interview. Indeed, in his obituary, the *Washington Post* noted: "Mr. Killebrew was known for his quiet amiability and was never ejected from a game in his 22-year career."

Chapter 4

BALTIMORE CHOPS

CHASING A-ROD'S 3,000TH HIT

Seth Hawkins is not a superfan. He's simply obsessed with milestones.

NEW YORKER, JUNE 2015

Introduction

I interviewed Seth Hawkins at his home in St. Paul, Minnesota, just across the river from my house in Minneapolis. He amused me the way he spoke of himself in the third person as "Dr. Fan" and with his reluctance to embrace modern amenities. I was further intrigued by the contrast of him celebrating the greatest achievements of baseball's best while simultaneously embracing James Garfield, long considered the worst of U.S. presidents.

Sometime this month, Alex Rodriguez is likely to get his 3,000th hit, becoming the 29th player in MLB history, and only the second Yankee, to reach the milestone. Whether it happens at Camden Yards in Baltimore, Marlins Park in Miami, or at home at Yankee Stadium, Seth Hawkins will be there. Hawkins has been there for each of the last 20 batters who have joined the 3,000-hit club, from Hank Aaron in 1970 to Derek Jeter four summers ago.

Hawkins, who is 72, grew up in Queens. A solitary and unathletic kid, he didn't play baseball. "My sport was chess," he said. But he listened to games on the tabletop radio in his living room, pulling in broadcasts from as far away as St. Louis and Chicago. "The whole league was available if you had a good radio." By age nine, he was riding the subway on his own to go to afternoon games at one of New York's three ballparks.

He credits his mother, a secretary for an insurance company, for his love of the game and for his appreciation of its history. The summer he turned 10, she took him to Boston to see a game at Braves Field before the team uprooted for Milwaukee.

That began a quest to visit all of the major-league ballparks. Since 1947, Hawkins has attended at least one regular-season game in every ballpark where MLB has played, including novelty sites in Honolulu, San Juan, and Tokyo.

His pursuit to be present at every 3,000th hit started with Hank Aaron and Willie Mays. When he realized that the two future Hall of Famers were on pace to reach the milestone during the same season in 1970, Hawkins resolved to witness both events. "I thought, even if I do nothing else, this is going to give me something to talk about," he said. "After that, I got infected with the three-thousand-hit bug, and decided to keep doing it."

Hawkins is a collector by nature, and is especially fond of the late nineteenth century. He has filled his house, a two-story Victorian on a quiet side street in St. Paul, with porcelain figurines shelved in a corner, black-and-white postcards mounted on a stereoscope, antique furniture, period wallpaper, and Turkish rugs, transforming it into a private museum that he calls the Julian H. Sleeper House, after the original owner, who built it in 1884. Hawkins, twice divorced, lives there with three cats and a life-size mannequin of President James A. Garfield.

Seated in the parlor next to a stuffed owl atop a Wooton desk, wearing a gray sport coat, a blue shirt, and a necktie decorated with baseballs, Hawkins speaks in full, indulgent paragraphs. He is accustomed to captive audiences, having taught communications for 35 years, the bulk of them at Southern Connecticut State University. Occasionally, he refers to himself in the third person, as Dr. Fan, the nickname given to him in 1985 by Bob McCoy in his *Sporting News* column.

In addition to the 3,000-hit games, Hawkins has witnessed some memorable bonus events: Mike Schmidt, Mark McGwire, and Sammy Sosa reaching 500 career home runs; Phil Niekro, Don Sutton, and Tom Glavine winning their 300th games; and Pete Rose notching hit No. 4,000, to name a few. He had set out to see Niekro deliberately, but the others happened by chance while he was after another one of his other collectables. But early on he decided to collect 3,000-hit milestones because they were predictable and infrequent enough to make advance travel arrangements possible. Hawkins has never owned a car or had a driver's license, so he has had to find other modes of transportation, from friends with cars to buses to planes and trains.

His strategy is to wait until a player gets within four or five hits and then start attending every game he plays until he reaches the milestone, which usually takes less than a week. Injuries can complicate plans, such as when George Brett, nearing the mark late in the 1992 season, sat out a couple of games nursing a sore shoulder. But Hawkins got a tip from someone he calls "an insider" that Brett was going to play in a road game against the Angels; he was able to get to Anaheim, where Brett had a four-hit day to reach the magic number.

The most serious threat to Hawkins's streak came in the summer of 1999, when Tony Gwynn, of the San Diego Padres, and Wade Boggs, of the Tampa Bay Devil Rays, closed in on their 3,000th hits simultaneously. "I started having nightmares a year in advance that they would do it on the same night in different cities," Hawkins said.

He scrutinized the box scores for both, watching their hit tallies rise, trying to predict when and where each player would reach his milestone. With Boggs at 2,999 on an off day in August, Hawkins saw Gwynn hit No. 2,999 in St. Louis then followed the Padres to Montreal. Hawkins got delayed at the airport and had to race to the ballpark. He bought a ticket on the street and had not been in his seat 10 minutes before Gwynn got his big hit.

Lucky for Hawkins, Boggs went 0-for-3 that same day. Hawkins headed back to the airport, found a flight from Montreal to Tampa via Cincinnati—this was back when you could buy an open ticket—and managed to see Boggs reach 3,000 the next night at Tropicana Field.

In the course of 45 years and 20 players, he's logged a lot of miles and spent at least six figures in his pursuit. "There were times I put up some large amounts on my Visa with expensive flights, but you do it because there's no second chance," he said.

Hawkins's unique pursuit has not gone unnoticed. In 2002, the Baseball Reliquary, an organization that honors the game's oddities and oddballs, bestowed him with its annual Hilda Award, named after Hilda Chester, famous for ringing her cowbell at Ebbets Field for 30 years. "Dr. Fan definitely comes out of that crazy and wacky tradition of fans who love the game and are obsessive about it," Terry Cannon, Baseball Reliquary's founder and keeper, said.

Hawkins calls the award, which he keeps in an upstairs bedroom stuffed with baseball memorabilia, his "greatest honor."

He has been recognized in other ways, too. When Rod Carew reached his milestone in Anaheim, Hawkins looked up to see himself pictured on the Jumbotron with a note about his accomplishment. (He had let the Angels management know that he would be there and what seat he was in.) Fans seated nearby started passing down their ticket stubs for Hawkins to autograph. "There were more than fifty for Dr. Fan to sign," Hawkins said.

Carew's is among his favorite milestone moments. Others include Gwynn, whose work ethic he admired; Craig Biggio, whom he found especially likable; and Cal Ripken Jr., who reached 3,000 at the Metrodome, a convenient eight-mile bus ride from Hawkins's house.

Now he is after Alex Rodriguez. Hawkins regards his latest quarry with the same dispassionate interest as the previous 20: despite having grown up in New York when the city hosted three ballclubs, he has never picked a favorite team to root for. "I'm as impartial as an umpire," he declared. "Baseball is certainly a religion for Dr. Fan, but it's not a religion where I worship a particular team." So when A-Rod reaches his milestone, Dr. Fan will be there as usual, scorecard in hand, sporting "a tasteful baseball cap without a logo, to show my neutrality."

Hawkins also remains neutral about Rodriguez's recent suspension for performance-enhancing drugs. "It's not my place for me to judge whether he's tainted or not," he said. "If Major League Baseball will accept his hits, I will, too. I will politely applaud him the way I have done the past twenty."

Dr. Fan plans to continue his pursuit for as long as his health allows. This could include 3,000th hits by Ichiro Suzuki, Adrián Beltré, and Albert Pujols over the next several years. Hawkins would especially like to see Ichiro, who has 2,878 hits, make the 3,000-hit club, perhaps sometime next season. "If he does it, he will instantly be Dr. Fan's favorite," Hawkins said. "As you can see, my mind is in the 1880s. Ichiro is a version of a nineteenth-century ballplayer come back to life. He's an improved version of Wee Willie Keeler"—the most prolific hitter of that era. "He's worth waiting for."

Postscript

Dr. Fan did indeed get to witness Alex Rodriguez's 3,000th hit on June 19, 2015. He was at Yankee Stadium with 44,587 others when Rodriguez lined Justin Verlander's 95-mph fastball over the right-field fence, only the third player in history to homer for his 3,000th hit. Coincidentally, the last player to reach 3,000, his teammate Derek Jeter, also did so with a home run.

Hawkins was also there to see the next three players enter the 3,000-hit club: Adrián Beltré on July 30, 2016, at Globe Life Park in Arlington; Ichiro Suzuki on August 7, 2016, at Coors Field in Denver; and Albert Pujols on May 4, 2018, at Safeco Field in Seattle. He's on deck for Miguel Cabrera, sitting at 2,866 hits after the 2020 season. "I'm even older than Joe Biden—by five months," he told me recently. "I have no intention to retire as Dr. Fan unless the medical community tells me Dr. Fan must hang it up."

THE IRREVERENT RELICS OF THE BASEBALL RELIQUARY

It's been called "the fans' Hall of Fame," "the antithesis of Cooperstown," and "the motherlode vein leading to the heart and soul of baseball." And yes, that's a jockstrap behind glass.

VICE SPORTS, AUGUST 2015

Introduction

I've got fellow SABR member Jon Leonoudakis to thank for introducing me to the Baseball Reliquary. Leonoudakis gave me a copy of his documentary *Not Exactly Cooperstown*, and soon as I watched it, I became an instant fan of the Baseball Reliquary. I had to write about this place.

It's hard to say where the Baseball Reliquary began. Maybe it started with a drop of Juan Marichal's sweat or Bill Veeck's autobiography. It might also have been a pubic hair purportedly belonging to St. Nick. Pinpointing its beginnings is as difficult as defining the Reliquary itself.

It's been called "the fans' Hall of Fame," "the antithesis of Cooperstown," and "the motherlode vein leading to the heart and soul of baseball." It calls itself "a nonprofit, educational organization dedicated to fostering an appreciation of American art and culture through the context of baseball history," but that doesn't really capture the Reliquary's unique nature. "It's hard to categorize," admits Terry Cannon, age 62, a part-time library assistant in Pasadena, California, who founded the Reliquary in 1996. "It's an amazing living organism in all of the directions it has moved into, but it retains the vision I started with."

Cannon's vision, to create an organization that embraced his dual passions for art and baseball, has evolved over the past two decades into a nomadic Hall of Fame that celebrates all that is wacky and wonderful about the national pastime. It stages four to six annual exhibits (mostly in Southern California libraries) from its collection of artifacts, ranging from Eddie Gaedel's jockstrap to a portrait of Dave Winfield constructed with chewed bubble gum. The Reliquary counts 51 honorees in its Shrine of the Eternals, including established mavericks like Bill Lee, Marvin Miller, Pete Rose, Jim Bouton, and the San Diego Chicken as well as lesser-knowns such as Steve Dalkowski (the hardest-throwing pitcher never to play in the major leagues) and Lester Rodney (the journalist who advocated for integration of Organized Baseball but was ostracized as a communist).

Exactly what you might expect from a man who was enamored of Bill Veeck's autobiography *Veeck as in Wreck* in 1963 when he read it as a 10-year-old. Veeck had Cannon from the first chapter, with his description of hiring the 3-foot-7 little person Gaedel to pinch-hit. "Eddie Gaedel was an assault on the baseball establishment," says Cannon, a self-confessed nonconformist. "I love that. Veeck's vision in terms of being a gadfly is a little of what I was looking to do with the Reliquary."

Cannon caught a whiff of the impression a good artifact could make three years later, when, at the first exhibition game the California Angels played at their new Anaheim Stadium, he spotted Giants pitcher Juan Marichal running sprints in the outfield and asked for an autograph. As Marichal signed Cannon's game program, a bead of sweat dripped from his forehead onto the page. Cannon marveled at how it dried the next day into a brown blotch. "I went around the neighborhood showing other kids—'This is Juan Marichal's sweat,'" Cannon says. "That could have been the beginning of the Reliquary, of gathering artifacts that tell stories."

Or at least it planted the seed, nurtured in later years by the Mardi Gras parties Cannon attended with his wife Mary. They dressed in costume, he as the pope wearing a miter decorated with baseball insignias; they carried bogus Vatican artifacts displayed in elegant boxes, such as the hair once adorning the holy pubis of Saint Nicholas. "We had a lot of fun with that," he says. "When I was starting the Baseball Reliquary and looking for a name, the way we planned to exhibit early items like a hot dog partially eaten by Babe Ruth didn't seem much of a stretch from what you would find of saints in the basements of Italian churches."

Cannon, an agnostic, did not grow up Catholic, but his wife did, and there are strong strains of Catholicism that run throughout the Reliquary, from its name to its memorabilia. Consider the tortilla imprinted with an image of Walter O'Malley's face (remind you of Veronica's cloth or a certain grilled cheese that made headlines not long ago?); a piece of skin supposedly taken from Abner Doubleday's thigh (similar to grafts and bone fragments populating those Italian church basements); and the panties that Wade Boggs insisted his mistress wear during his hitting streak (granted, no parallel there in Catholic tradition). The organization does not go in for piety; rather, the Reliquary revels in irreverence, very much in the spirit of Veeck, its "spiritual guru."

The Reliquary website proclaims that it "gladly accepts the donation of artworks and objects of historic content, provided their authenticity is well documented." Cannon admits this is more a jab at the memorabilia craze, which he finds "laughable," "ridiculous," and "obscene," with values of legitimate objects of interest artificially propped up by auction houses. "Our objects offer a counterpoint to that," he says. "We don't really care about their 'authenticity,' because we're more interested in an object's ability to convey a story."

He points to the O'Malley tortilla for the way it conveys the story of Chavez Ravine. The city of Los Angeles evicted poor residents, many of them Mexican American, in order to build Dodger Stadium; it's one of the most egregious uses of eminent domain on record, but history has wrongly assigned O'Malley the blame. In fact, Cannon explains, when O'Malley found out what had happened on the site where he wanted to build Dodger Stadium, he offered the few remaining residents compensation that exceeded the actual value of their property for them to relocate. "This item resonates because it's unique and is a powerful way to tell the story," Cannon says.

Additional relics in the collection include baseballs autographed by Mother Teresa, a rubber model of Mordecai Brown's missing finger, Dock Ellis's hair curlers, a Charlie Finley orange baseball, and one of Cannon's favorites: a hunk of dirt from Elysian Fields, site of the first recorded game of Organized Baseball, played in 1846. He received it from the great-great-great-grandson of James Orr. Orr, a poet, supposedly dug up the soil surreptitiously after being moved by watching a game played there and predicting that baseball would become a grand and noble sport. "That's an important artifact," Cannon says. "It was dug up and conserved by a man of incredible vision. It ties in the idea of baseball and poetry, baseball and art. We're always seeking that out."

He's serious when he says that. Indeed, the Reliquary has a scholarly bent, making its expansive archives available to the public through the Institute for Baseball Studies hosted by Whittier College in Southern California and the Latino Baseball History Project, a collaboration with California State University, San Bernardino, that documents baseball's social and cultural significance in the Latino community.

Three years after founding the Reliquary, Cannon added the Shrine of the Eternals in 1999. Where members of the Baseball Writers' Association of America select inductees into the National Baseball Hall of Fame primarily on the basis of statistics, the Reliquary general membership votes on eternals who animated the game and entertained fans with their colorful personalities. There's very little overlap in the two pantheons' membership; Yogi Berra, Dizzy Dean, Josh Gibson, Satchel Paige, Jackie Robinson, and Casey Stengel are the only people enshrined in both. Veeck, Ellis, and Curt Flood made up the first class of eternals.

For many of those selected, it is the first time they have been recognized in a positive way for their contribution to baseball. As a result, the induction ceremony can become an emotional experience. Ellis, who allegedly pitched a no-hitter while tripping on acid and anonymously spent much of his retirement doing social work, broke down while accepting his award. "I realized right then and there that we were going to be successful," Cannon says. "Because we were honoring people who hadn't been honored elsewhere."

This year marked the 17th annual Shrine of the Eternals Induction Day. On Sunday, July 19, Cannon kicked off over two hours of festivities by raising an oversize cowbell and, just as Hilda Chester used to do at Ebbets Field, clanging it over his head. Audience members joined with their collection of bells to rattle the halls of the Pasadena Central Library for nearly a half minute. After some introductory remarks, Cannon asked the 200 or so people present to rise for the traditional—at least in the Reliquary sense—singing of the national anthem and introduced Jackie Lee. An 82-year-old woman dressed in a skimpy gold lamé leotard walked onto the stage, where she stood on her head, splaying her long white hair across the hardwood floor, and started to sing in a quavering soprano, "Oh, say can you see . . ."

With moments alternately humorous, serious, and poignant, the ceremony was devoted to stories, mostly obscure, about this year's award recipients. As a warm-up, Cannon presented the Hilda Award to Tom Keefe, founder of the Eddie Gaedel Society, and the Tony Salin Memorial Award to Gary Joseph Cieradkowski for his "commitment to the preservation of baseball history" in creating the *Infinite Baseball Card Set* blog.

The meat and potatoes of the event came with the presentations and acceptances of this year's three inductees into the Shrine of the Eternals: Sy Berger, the "Father of the Modern Baseball Card" who designed Topps' 1952 line of cards; Glenn Burke, MLB's first gay pioneer, closeted to the public but open with his teammates during four years with the Dodgers and A's; and Steve Bilko, a slugging star and strikeout king (as a batter) for the Los Angeles Angels during the denouement of the Pacific Coast League.

Berger's son Glen gave an entertaining introductory speech spiked with name-dropping anecdotes about his father with Willie Mays, George Steinbrenner, and Brian Epstein (yes, that one, the Beatles' manager). A five-minute video clip introduced Glenn Burke. Folk singer Ross Altman sang a tribute to Bilko with his harmonica and acoustic guitar: "When that bat connected, it was music to our ears / Just like the Babe before him, he put them in the stratosphere."

Membership in the Reliquary is open to anyone willing to pay $25 in annual dues. There are nearly 300 such people, and their money, along with a small annual grant from the Los Angeles County Arts Commission, comprises the budget, which doesn't always cover travel expenses for inductees and speaker stipends. Since all Reliquary events are free, the primary perk of membership is being able to vote in the annual election of inductees into the Shrine of the Eternals.

There are other, less tangible benefits of membership. Jon Leonoudakis, a producer who has made TV commercials for clients such as Honda and interactive displays for theme parks like Disneyland, attended his first Reliquary induction ceremony in 2002. Leonoudakis has been a baseball fan since he was five years old, but had become disillusioned by steroid use and corporatization of the game. Watching the Reliquary induct Mark Fidrych, Shoeless Joe Jackson, and Minnie Miñoso into its shrine, he says, reignited his love of the game. "The vibe and the crowd—there was a guy dressed in full 1919 regalia—launched me into the stratosphere of fandom," he says. "It totally changed the journey of my life."

Leonoudakis resolved to make documentaries that told the story of the game and started, naturally, with one about the Reliquary, titled *Not Exactly Cooperstown*, released in 2012. He's currently finishing a film about Arnold Hano, the prolific baseball writer and 2010 recipient of the Reliquary's Hilda Award, given to recognize distinguished service to the game by a baseball fan. Other recipients of what Cannon calls "the baseball fans' equivalent of the Oscar or Emmy" include Bill Murray and Sister Mary Assumpta Zabas, who has baked cookies for Cleveland Indians players since 1984. "The Reliquary is the only Hall of Fame where the fans get to vote," Leonoudakis says. "They embrace the fans' importance and recognize fandom is the lifeblood of the game."

Postscript

It was a sad day for baseball fans when Terry Cannon passed away on August 1, 2020, from bile duct cancer at 66. "Terry Cannon touched the lives of many with his kindness, generosity, humor and a sprinkle of mischievousness," read his obituary in the *Pasadena Star-News*. "He brought people together from all walks of life, and made the world a richer place."

By the time of Cannon's death, membership in the Shrine of the Eternals had grown to 66 members with 15 inductees since the publication of this article: Billy Beane, Charlie Brown, Bob Costas, Nancy Faust, Lisa Fernandez, Rube Foster, Arnold Hano, Bo Jackson, Tommy John, Don Newcombe, Max Patkin, J. R. Richard, Vin Scully, Rusty Staub, and Bob Uecker.

Leonoudakis released *Hano! A Century in the Bleachers* in 2015. He had made another documentary that debuted in 2014: *The Day the World Series Stopped*, about the earthquake that interrupted Game Three of the 1989 World Series at Candlestick Park. He also produced *The Sweet Spot: A Treasury of Baseball Stories*, a baseball documentary anthology series on Amazon Prime that debuted in 2016. In 2020, he released three films: *108 Stitches*, *Mudcat Grant's Pitching Secrets*, and *Consider the Source: A Visit with Greg Goossen*.

A GAME OF THEIR OWN

They play the national pastime a little differently in Lake Tomahawk, Wisconsin, world's capital of snowshoe baseball.

SPORTS ON EARTH, JULY 2014

Introduction

While researching an article about outdoor festivals in Milwaukee, I came across the town of Lake Tomahawk, Wisconsin, "world's capital of snowshoe baseball." That got my attention. I called the Lake Tomahawk Chamber of Commerce. They directed me to Frank Christianson, a retired town road maintenance worker. "Yep," Christianson confirmed. "We play baseball on snowshoes. In the summertime."

"But . . . there's no snow then," I said.

"We spread sawdust across the infield," he said.

"What about the outfield?"

"It's just gravel. You can tell the outfielders—they're the ones with the scraped elbows."

This I had to see. I landed an assignment from *Sports Illustrated* to write a short item for the Scorecard department about Lake Tomahawk's take on the national pastime.

When I pulled into town on a July evening in 1999, I saw the marquee outside the chamber: "Snowshoe Baseball: Sports Illustrated Night." Frank and company were very gracious. They even let me take a turn at bat with the snowshoes on (and, of course, I nearly did a faceplant trying to run out a groundball). Afterward they wanted to buy me drinks in the bar. I think they thought I was writing a cover story.

Broke my heart when the editor decided not to run my piece; I knew they were going to be disappointed in Lake Tomahawk. (The editor said he liked it, but he typically overassigned items so he wouldn't be caught short.) Frank took it well when I told him the news, but what they were doing in Lake Tomahawk stayed with me, and even after Christianson passed away, I still felt I owed it to him to write a proper article about snowshoe baseball in Lake Tomahawk. Fifteen years later, I returned on assignment for *Sports on Earth*.

They play the national pastime a little differently here—on snowshoes. In the summertime. The local team has a decided home-field advantage, having learned to shuffle along the eight inches of coarse sawdust spread throughout the infield. On this particular Monday evening in July, Don Hilgendorf, 76, a retired Division III baseball coach and the driving force behind this unique brand of entertainment, gathers his players for a pregame pep talk.

The only team to beat his Snow Hawks in recent years has been that night's opponent, the Chicago All-Stars, who swept a two-game series last summer and won a special July 4 contest the previous Friday, 10–9. "You remember what happened last year," Hilgendorf tells the 14 players on snowshoes gathered around him. "We don't want that to happen again."

From his second-floor perch behind home plate, the public address announcer, Jim Soyck, 79, the voice of snowshoe baseball—and an unapologetic homer who calls strikes for the Snow Hawks' pitcher, compliments hometown fielders, and exhorts the hitters to rally—ups the ante with his pregame announcement: "We are out for a little revenge tonight. I've got a ten-dollar bet on our guys."

Soyck and the crowd of 1,000, approximately the population of Lake Tomahawk, cheer the Snow Hawks' early 1–0 lead. They spread beyond the bleachers in their lawn chairs along both foul lines and sit on the grass beyond the right-field fence. Some of these people stopped by as early as 6:00 A.M. that morning to reserve bleacher seats with blankets, a time-honored tradition. (For the July 4 game earlier that weekend, when the crowd pushed 3,000, they staked their seats out two days in advance.) Admission is free. "This is the big thing in Lake Tomahawk in summertime," Soyck says.

It's true. There's not much else competing for entertainment on Monday nights in Lake Tomahawk, a pause along State Highway 47 of four bars, several other establishments, and no stoplight in the Northwoods. Indeed, the local area television station reports on the games and even puts together a team to challenge the Snow Hawks annually. Many of the fans arrive more than two hours before the 7:30 P.M. start for the pregame cookout hosted in the adjacent pavilion by one of eight local service organizations serving brats, burgers, hot dogs, soda, and pie slices. The pies are the big draw. This evening there are 83 of more than three dozen varieties, all homemade by the ladies of the American Legion post, selling for a dollar a slice. (On July 4, they sold out slices from 159 pies before the game was half over.)

Welcome to a place that Norman Rockwell would envy.

* * *

They've been playing snowshoe baseball for more than half a century in "Lake Tom." It began in a more traditional fashion, playing on snowshoes in the wintertime with a ball painted red so they could find it in the snow. Snowshoe baseball flourished in the area during the 1990s when there were about 40 sponsored teams representing every small town in this resort area. But as players retired and fans yielded to windchills, the winter game withered. No matter, because by then the summer version had flourished. Back in 1961, town chairman Roy Sloan had the vision to replicate snow with coarse sawdust in a park a block off the main strip so they could play in warmer weather. The unusual attraction distinguished Lake Tomahawk from the water ski shows prevalent in surrounding resort communities and caught on. This year, with games played every Monday from June 20 to August 29, marks the 53rd summer season.

Hilgendorf expanded the spectacle when he took over in 1998. He raised the funds to replace the rickety press box behind home plate with a solid two-story concrete structure, refit the bleachers with aluminum benches, replaced the decrepit backstop with chain-link, erected bright new lights, built comfortable restrooms, and updated the food service in the pavilion, which used to stretch a hose from a neighboring house for running water. Most significantly, he elevated the quality of play. Back in the day, the visiting team felt like the Washington Generals, giving away games to please the home crowd. But Hilgendorf scoured the area for players with talent, assembling a group of young guys driven to win. "We used to think of it as kind of a joke, but the fans were really into it, so we figured if they're taking it that seriously, we better take it seriously," says Snow Hawks third baseman Jeff Smith, who has been playing 10 years.

The improvements have similarly enhanced the crowds. Over the past 15 years, the number of fans has nearly tripled. Some fans have been coming regularly for 20 years or longer. Then there are those who've gotten the bug more recently, like Barbara and Gerry Brahm, a retired couple from Milwaukee with a house in the area. They started coming four years ago to watch their granddaughter's boyfriend play. The granddaughter has since married the ballplayer, who no longer plays, but Barbara and Gerry remain regular fans. "It's crazy to watch," Gerry says, gobbling a piece of pie before the game. "It's a fun game. They're not out for blood."

*   *   *

The Chicago All-Stars have got game. They're led by Dave Maize, who played four years in the Pittsburgh Pirates' farm system, rising as far as Triple A. Now a keg-shaped, 43-year-old cop in Glenview, Illinois, he's still got soft hands, a strong arm, and a powerful swing. He's the only guy Hilgendorf has seen hit a ball onto the roof of the American Legion post in left field—a feat Maize has accomplished twice.

Maize has put together what could more aptly be called an all-family team with his two brothers, a pair of cousins and their two sons, rounded out by a couple of friends, almost all of them softball players back home. They have made it an annual tradition to bring their family up for the weekend, camping out at the Maize parents' home.

The locals appreciate the economic boost the nearly three dozen guests bring to the area, spending money on food, beer, and gas in town. Before the game, Soyck, who owns Jimmy's Happy Daze bar along the main drag, singled out Judy Maize, the family matriarch, announced it was her birthday, and led the crowd in a chorus of "Happy Birthday."

Maize and his boys can hit—they score six runs in the top of the second inning to take a 6–1 lead—but they stumble some in the field, and the Snow Hawks notch three runs in their half, a couple on errors, to narrow the lead to 6–4.

Tod Niemuth scores one of those runs, dropping a blooper in front of Maize in left field for a base hit and later scooting home on another hit with an aggressive bit of baserunning, sliding into home head first. You can't slide feet first—you'll bust up your snowshoes or they'll smack you in the face.

When Niemuth bats again, Hilgendorf, sharing the PA duties with Soyck, tells the crowd, "Tod is one of the youngest players on the Snow Hawks. He's 57." Niemuth grins. He's actually 58, the oldest guy by eight years, having played with some of his teammates' fathers, but still wiry and fit. Niemuth's own dad played—he's one of a half dozen of second-generation players on the current Snow Hawks ("It's in our blood," he says). Niemuth made his debut when he was 14. Having slowed some over the ensuing 44 years, he has ceded the outfield to younger players and taken up residence at first base, where he has endured plenty of jammed thumbs and dislocated fingers, but he has no plans to retire. "It [snowshoe baseball] has been in my lifestyle since I was a kid," Niemuth says. "I never grew out of it. As long as I'm still healthy, I'll keep doing it. I guess it's sort of an addiction."

*   *   *

Just to clarify, they're not actually playing baseball; they use a 16-inch softball without gloves, which explains the jammed and dislocated digits. The snowshoe part is for real, though, each player outfitted with a pair of oval-shaped, wood and rawhide, 30-inch-long Bear Paw shoes. "The trick is being able to run in snowshoes," Niemuth says. "For some people, it's as simple as putting on a pair of gloves." For the others? "It's not uncommon to see them falling on the way to first base."

After a few years acclimating to the snowshoes, the Chicago All-Stars move pretty well this evening, though their shortstop takes several tumbles in the field, and one baserunner gets tangled up trying to beat out a ground-ball to first base, belly flopping into the sawdust. Meanwhile, some of the Lake Tomahawk players glide so gracefully across the field and basepaths that it's easy to forget they're shod with an impediment. Yet they're equally imperiled. When the left-center fielder (they play nine in the field plus a catcher) races back for a drive, he catches it over his shoulder, stumbles slightly, and takes several strides to steady himself beyond where the sawdust is spread. The crowd sends up a hearty ovation as much for his athletic catch as for his ability to avoid a nasty scrape on the gravel.

*   *   *

After four innings, the Snow Hawks are ahead 7–6. The Chicago All-Stars score two to go up 8–7, but the local team rallies again to reclaim the lead, 10–8. That's where the score stands, top of the seventh, when the first Chicago batter, Patrick O'Gara, strides to the plate. The 43-year-old pipefitter by day senses what's up—the home team's about to serve up a Globetrotteresque gag. He goes along with it, takes a mighty cut at a muskmelon painted yellow like a regular ball, and splatters the melon guts all over himself, the catcher, and the ump. The crowd laughs, like they're seeing this for the first time even though it's been a staple of the Monday night game for decades. "You gotta swing," O'Gara says afterward. "A melon hitting the ground isn't any fun for the fans to watch, so you swing as hard as you possibly can."

The Chicago crew picks up their play in the field, nearly turning a 6-4-3-2 triple play, but the runner slides in safely (head first, of course), beating the throw home. That sustains another Snow Hawks rally that sends the score to 16–8, which is where it remains until the final out, when Niemuth squeezes a throw from the pitcher to complete a 1-3 play.

The players line up to shake hands, pose for a photo together, share some laughs with the fans, and retire to the "afterglow," as much a part of the Monday night routine as the pies and muskmelon. This evening, fans and players from both teams rehash the game over pizza and pitchers of beer at the Shamrock bar two blocks from the field.

Niemuth outdid Maize, reaching safely in each of his four at-bats, including smacking two doubles and scoring three runs. The Snow Hawks exacted their revenge after Friday night's defeat, reasserting their dominance, and Jim Soyck won his bet. But if you didn't know the final score, you would have thought the Chicago side won from looking at Patrick O'Gara. The sweat has soaked through the shoulders of his T-shirt, but he's all smiles. "This crowd is huge for a goofy game in the park," he says. "It doesn't get any better than that."

Postscript

I was a little sheepish about going back to Lake Tomahawk after letting them down following "Sports Illustrated Night." But the people there were very gracious to me, and once again, it was an entertaining evening. Should you ever find yourselves in the Rhinelander area of Wisconsin on a summer evening when they're playing snowshoe baseball, I recommend you stop to check it out.

TAKE ME OUT TO THE OLD BALLGAME

Forget what you've heard about Abner Doubleday. The Vintage Base Ball Association plays to set the record straight.

HISTORY CHANNEL MAGAZINE, JULY/AUGUST 2012

Introduction

I'd been hearing from some members in my local SABR chapter about vintage baseball, so I was happy to have the chance to learn more about the way the game was played with this assignment for the *History Channel Magazine,* especially since it involved the chance to interview the idiosyncratic and ever-entertaining Jim Bouton.

Picture a field on a summer afternoon. Nine men a side dressed in solid-colored trousers, blousy tops, and small-brimmed caps. The man in the center tosses a ball underhand to a batsman 45 feet away. The catcher stands half a dozen feet back, barehanded. The batsman swings his thick lumber, cracks the ball to left field, and legs it to a canvas bag stuffed with sawdust. The fielder, also barehanded, catches the ball on one bounce. Out!

This could be almost any American town circa 1863, but it's actually North Oaks, Minnesota, June 26, 2011. The Stillwater Quicksteps take on the North Oaks Fighting Buckthorn as part of the Hill Farms Historical Society Ice Cream Social festivities. The Quicksteps, composed of baseball historians who are members of the Twin Cities chapter of the Society for American Baseball Research, play the national pastime the way it used to be played. Forget that hooey you learned about Abner Doubleday inventing baseball; they aim to set the record straight with their replication.

The Quicksteps are one of 78 clubs across the country in the Vintage Base Ball Association playing variations of nineteenth-century base ball (it wasn't spelled as one word until the 1880s). They do so at ice cream socials, town festivals, historic preservations, county fairs, even in exhibitions before MLB games in Minneapolis, Boston, Cincinnati, Cleveland, and San Francisco, "to preserve, perpetuate, and promote the game of base ball as it was played during its formative years in the nineteenth century." The game's an animated history lesson, fruit of their research, intended to portray the authenticity of the national pastime.

"Our mission is to recreate the game in as historically accurate manner as we can, trying to educate the public and disseminate info as it was actually played in formative years," says Paul Salamone, VBBA vice president and first baseman for the Elizabeth Resolutes in New Jersey.

While vintage base ball shares the basics with the modern game—nine fielders, four bases, three outs a side, a batter swinging at a pitched ball—there are distinctive differences that make the old game look different, beyond the hand-stitched uniforms. Before 1865, a batted ball—fair or foul—caught on one bounce was an out. The batsman—or striker—could request where he wanted the ball pitched and wait until the pitcher put it there without the lone umpire calling balls and strikes, though the umpire may eventually issue the warning, "Ball to plate, sir." The pitcher threw underhand without a windup or bending his arm from a flat area (the mound didn't arrive until 1893) 45 feet from home base. There were no outfield fences, hence no automatic home runs. The bats had thicker handles, and the balls were slightly bigger (between 9 3/4 and 10 inches in circumference compared to the modern ball between 9 and 9 1/4 inches). Players did not wear gloves until the 1880s. Runners could not overrun first base with impunity.

Many teams play by the rules of 1864, but some play by rules specific to other years. For instance, Salamone's team, the Resolutes, play by 1873 rules, when the ball had to be caught on the fly to be an out and runners could safely overrun first base. Though the rules vary by the year, the teams strive to be faithful to the rules of the specific time period they're replicating.

With some deliberate exceptions. In the 1860s, runners attempted steals on nearly every pitch, but today's vintage players limit the basestealing to keep fans interested. They also don't slide—mostly to avoid injury—because back in the day players only slid head first. "We bend the rules a bit," admits Rich Arpi, VBBA treasurer and Quicksteps captain. "Mostly as a concession to our age."

Baseball in the nineteenth century was a gentlemanly game. Players resolved disputes among themselves without the umpire intervening. They showed one another and the spectators courtesy. They behaved modestly. Those playing vintage base ball today mimic those aspects of the game as well. "There are no batting gloves, helmets, wrist bands, elbow pads, pajama pants, sunglasses, gold chains, earrings, logo shoes," says Jim Bouton, the former Yankees pitcher who became attracted to vintage base ball in an effort to save a historic ballpark near his Massachusetts home in 2004. "There's no high-fiving, trash-talking, pointing to the sky, or kissing jewelry. It's just baseball. It's purer."

* * *

The history of old rules baseball dates back 30 years to Long Island where the first games were played—or, replayed—at Old Bethpage Village Restoration in 1980. At about the same time, Ohio Village in Columbus, Ohio, played old-rules games independent of the New York historical group. Word spread, and teams began to sprout in other areas of the country. The term "vintage base ball" was coined in the 1990s by a group that eventually formed the Vintage Base Ball Association in 1996.

Salamone, a jazz pianist and music teacher living in Westfield, New Jersey, heard about vintage base ball from a program on his local public television station. He had played Little League baseball and wanted to get back into the game. Softball didn't appeal to him—"too watered down for my tastes." He worked out with a hardball team but decided to form his own vintage team, attracted by the idea of researching old-time base ball in his area. Thus, he reincarnated the Elizabeth Resolutes, the New Jersey state champions from 1870.

After almost a year, he had rounded up a dozen players, and the Resolutes began play in 2000 against other teams in the area. They usually play doubleheaders, one game by the Resolutes' 1873 rules, the second by the rules of the other team. Either way, Salamone and the others can't play the game the way they used to. Without a mitt at first base, Salamone has had to make adjustments. "When a guy fires the ball across the diamond, you may have to come off the base to catch it two-handed, then beat the runner to the base or tag him," says Salamone, 54. "You have to relearn the game." Even so, the jazz pianist has nursed his share of bruised fingers and a broken wrist.

When a neighbor invited Scott Westgate to join his vintage team shortly after Westgate moved to Rochester, Michigan, in 2003, Westgate balked. He had played four years of high school baseball and a semester of Division II college ball as a pitcher and first baseman. "When I found out they played barehanded hardball, I wondered what kind of quality baseball can this be," says Westgate, 48, who owns a pension consulting firm.

Still, figuring it would be a good way to get to know some people in his new community, he agreed to give the game a try—and was pleasantly surprised. Sure, there were some septuagenarians indulging dreams that wouldn't die, but there were also guys in their 20s with baseball pedigrees. "I found out there are some ballplayers who can really play," he says.

Westgate was soon pitching regularly for the Rochester Grangers. "It's really addicting," he says.

The camaraderie drew him in, as it does many baseball fans. "Not only the camaraderie of my teammates, but of the baseball community in general," says Westgate, who currently serves as VBBA president. "I'm meeting people from New York, Minnesota, Colorado, Arizona. It's a common bond. It's fun."

Rich Arpi, a historian who had enjoyed sandlot ball, jumped at the chance to take the field again "at a level I could play." Now the Quicksteps captain, the 55-year-old has been playing for 20 years, most recently for the Quicksteps and the St. Croix Base Ball Club in Minnesota. "People make baserunning mistakes, fielding errors, but nobody yells at you," he says. "There's not the pressure to win."

That's in large part because of the emphasis on base ball as a gentleman's game. But that's not to say players don't want to win. "We don't do it for the competition, though the boy in us wants to win every game if we're playing a game," Westgate admits.

It's not just boys swinging the old-fashioned bats—women have gotten involved as well during the past decade. Just as women played base ball as early as 1866—documented in a letter about the Vassar College club—so have they begun playing the vintage game, with teams such as the Ohio Village Diamonds, the Lady Clodbusters, the Lady Locks, the Hens, and others.

*   *   *

In his effort to save the historic Wahconah Park in Pittsfield, Massachusetts, Jim Bouton staged a vintage game in 2004 that ESPN Classic broadcast live. The popularity of the event inspired him to form the Vintage Base Ball Federation two years later along with sportswriter Frank Deford and baseball historian John Thorn. Teams in the VBBF play by post-1880 rules, which means gloves, overhand pitching, and called balls and strikes. They wear old-fashioned uniforms with knickers and colored socks. The federation planned to stage an annual six-team World Series tournament, though it has held only two in the half dozen years since its inception. Many of the players on the 40-odd VBBF clubs around the country played competitive ball at least at the high school level, and the median age skews younger than in the counterpart VBBA. "The 1860s game is played by historians who like baseball," says Bouton, who throws his knuckleball for the Whately (Massachusetts) Pioneers. "The 1880s teams are more baseball players who like history."

The VBBF, whose mission is "to spread the charms and values of vintage base ball, and accelerate the formation of vintage clubs and leagues around the world," has drawn criticism from the historians of the VBBA devoted to researching and replicating authentic vintage ball. They charge that the VBBF teams play by a compilation of nineteenth- and twentieth-century rules that misrepresents the game as it was. "It's not historically factual," Salamone says. "They are setting back research probably twenty years by presenting to the public a game that is completely fabricated."

Bouton, VBBF president, counters that the controversy today reflects what happened in the nineteenth century, when the rules of play were being debated and evolving, often by players on the field during a game. "The argument over who's playing by the proper rules that you see today in vintage base ball exactly mimics the arguments that were taking place in the 1800s," he says. "The arguments themselves are historically accurate."

Those dedicated to historical authenticity also suspect that Bouton's primary interest in the old game is financial. They point to the $500 annual fee he charges VBBF clubs. By contrast, clubs in the nonprofit VBBA pay a $50 membership fee. Yet, here, too, Bouton may be in step with the times—in the late 1860s, ballclubs began enclosing the fields with fences and charging admission. "They realized they could make a little money off of it," Arpi says. "That's when professional teams started taking over."

* * *

The fans seem to enjoy it either way. The vintage games give them a chance to step back in time to watch the national pastime as their great-great-great-grandparents may have seen it. Bouton and the others can agree that old-fashioned base ball has its place in modern times as a family spectacle. "It's a great family event because children watch it and have all kinds of questions," Bouton says. "It gives parents a nice chance to teach about manners and history."

For Arpi, the historian, that's the most satisfying part of playing vintage base ball. "I'm gratified when a father or mother with young children come up and ask questions," he says. "It gets them involved in the history of the game."

Postscript

A decade after this article first appeared, the Vintage Base Ball Association continues to thrive, now with more than 200 teams across the country. The Vintage Base Ball Federation, on the other hand, has not been active since 2017. Jim Bouton suffered a stroke in 2012 and never completely recovered. The pitcher who gained everlasting fame with his memoir *Ball Four* passed away July 10, 2019, at the age of 80.

Chapter 5

FOR LOVE OF THE GAME

COOPERSTOWN OR BUST

My last wish before he died was to make the pilgrimage with my dad to baseball's mecca.

MEMORIES & DREAMS, SUMMER 2019

Introduction

When the editor of *Memories & Dreams* told me they were devoting an issue to road trips, I knew right away the story I wanted to tell.

The summer before he died, my dad granted me one final memory: a weekend at the National Baseball Hall of Fame. I knew he had always wanted to go there but now, being sick, he wouldn't do it without a nudge. I also wanted the chance to make this one final special trip with him. Even though the cancer had weakened him, he obliged.

So in 2005, like countless other fathers and sons, we traveled to Cooperstown, the first time for both of us. We flew from Minneapolis into Albany because it was the closest airport and rented a car to drive the balance of 70 miles. There used to be a train that players took to Cooperstown for exhibition games and induction ceremonies, but that's no longer an option. Any journey these days to the Hall of Fame has the element of a road trip because even if you fly—to Albany, Hartford, or Rochester—you have to drive the rest of the way.

Dad drove, because he always did. He had driven me to the Met in the 1970s when he would go to the Twins office downtown the day tickets went on sale and buy a pair for each of their scheduled doubleheaders. He had driven to County Stadium in Milwaukee and to Comiskey and Wrigley in Chicago in the 1980s so we could watch baseball outdoors on grass after Calvin Griffith (temporarily) ruined the game with the Metrodome. To Kansas City and Kauffman Stadium in the 1990s, where we reminisced about the foul ball hit by George Brett that I had snagged years earlier at the Met, the only ball I ever caught even though I'd faithfully brought my glove to games.

Baseball had been our thing. Dad had passed on his love of the game to me. I remember him pitching a Wiffle ball to me when I was four years old in our suburban street (in the same neighborhood where Billy Martin lived in the 1960s when he was coaching then managing the Twins; Dad told me how he waited with Martin at the bus stop but didn't talk to him), playing catch in the yard with a real baseball when I got older, and him going to my games when we started wearing full uniforms. But it was at the ballparks where the love took root through baseball's oral tradition.

The pace of the game allows for fathers to pass along to sons the stories, explain the traditions, and explore the collective memory. Between pitches and between innings, he told me how for a dime and a Wheaties box top he sat with other kids on the warning track at Minneapolis Millers games. He loved to recall how Ray Dandridge, the Millers' African American third baseman, would toy with runners: either lobbing balls that he had timed perfectly to reach the first baseman's mitt an instant before the runner's foot touched the bag or scooping up a hard-hit groundball, eyeing the runner, and waiting, waiting—before rifling a throw to first that barely nipped him.

When we finally made it to the red brick building at 25 Main Street, we discovered it was a repository for all of those memories. In the Plaque Gallery, Dad immediately hunted down his hero, Ted Williams. Dad, who had fulfilled his ROTC obligation with two years in the navy, had deep respect for Williams as a hitter and a war hero. He'd told me many times about Williams's two tours of duty as a pilot and how his 521 career home runs could easily have been more than Willie Mays's 660 if he hadn't skipped almost five seasons serving his country. As a boy, Dad had taken the train to Chicago to see him play once at Comiskey. The Splendid Splinter made an indelible impression that day with a home run. Dad had never seen a more beautiful swing, a more graceful and gifted batter.

What about Rod Carew? I had gone straight to his plaque. Carew had been *my* boyhood hero, with his ability to bunt for base hits, to slap the ball to any field, and with that wonderful stance we loved to imitate. He animated the summer of 1977 with excitement when he chased .400 and became my sentimental favorite as the greatest hitter. Dad reminded me—after Carew finished at .388—how Williams had refused to sit out to protect his average and actually raised it to .406, going 6-for-8 in the doubleheader in Philadelphia on the last day of the 1941 season. No one, of course, has hit .400 since.

In the "Baseball at the Movies" room, the *Field of Dreams* poster caught my eye. During my teens and 20s, I rebelled and we clashed. We argued about sex, religion, and politics. I went the liberal route; Dad remained a steadfast conservative. Baseball served as our demilitarized zone. We shared mutual joy when the Twins won the World Series in 1987 and again in 1991. But we had caused collateral damage in between. So when I saw *Field of Dreams*, Kevin Costner's character making peace with his father inspired me to call mine and invite him to see the movie with me. Afterward, I apologized for the things I'd done or said that had been hurtful; Dad said he forgave me. Then he apologized, and I forgave him. We hugged and didn't need to say any more.

On the third floor, we watched the Abbott and Costello routine of "Who's on first?" Dad had told me about it, but I'd never seen it performed. We shared a laugh. I was able to understand his appreciation of the comedy duo.

In a souvenir shop across the street, when he saw me admiring a Bench T-shirt, Dad bought it for me. A catcher in my youth, I had admired Johnny Bench, hung a poster of him on my bedroom wall, and worn No. 5. I immediately put on the shirt. Dad bought himself a Hall of Fame cap he wore the rest of the trip.

The museum and sightseeing had worn out Dad. He asked to go back to the motel to take a nap. Dad was the kind of guy who never got sick, never missed a day of work. He'd made an appointment thinking he had a hernia, and the doctor discovered a tumor the size of a softball growing on his kidney. Later that month, after surgery at the Mayo Clinic, the surgeon informed our family that according to their database, it looked like my dad likely had three years to live. That had been two years ago.

Dad was a stoic Swede raised during the Depression among a generation of men who didn't talk about their troubles, let alone their emotions. When I'd ask how he was doing, he would reply, "All right, I guess," and change the subject. When he had told me on the flight that he was taking an experimental drug, it was my first hint how serious his condition had become—and how scared he might be.

We ate dinner that night on the Otesaga Hotel porch, with its picturesque view of the lake stretching between wooden hillsides. He had trouble swallowing his food. His terminal disease sat between us. What is it like to face death? I wanted to ask him. But it was not the kind of thing we talked about. Instead, we reminisced about the day: the introductory movie that gave us chills, the Babe Ruth exhibit, the team lockers, the Honus Wagner card, the statues of Hilda Chester and other early superfans—on through dessert.

We spent two more days touring the museum and town. I loved that everywhere we saw people wearing T-shirts or hats of their favorite teams. We had all been drawn there by our mutual love of baseball. Even among strangers, we knew we shared that bond. We treasured the memories the game had given us. In the end, I think what we love about the game goes beyond the numbers; it's the way the players made us feel—the thrill of watching Rod Carew beat out a bunt or Ted Williams deliver a home run, the feeling of identification with a player in handling his baseball card or wearing his number. The measure of a ballplayer is the depth of those memories he's generated in his career. Those who have given us the most end up in the Hall of Fame.

As we pulled out of Cooperstown and began weaving along the shore of Lake Otsego on our way back to Albany, I was grateful for the chance to have visited the mecca of those memories. And more so, to have done so with my father. Because the measure of a man is the same as that of a player: the depth of the memories he's imprinted on others. On our way out of town, I knew that we had given each other one more memory with our trip.

Postscript

I've been fortunate to return to Cooperstown a number of times since that first trip. Several times, it was to research or promote my baseball books. Once it was a trip with my wife and our two kids in October when the hillsides covered with fall colors were spectacular. Another time was in 2014, for Induction Weekend, with my son Brendan, who was 12 years old at the time. I hope he treasures the memories of that trip the way I do the one I made with my dad.

MY FATHER'S GLOVE

After my father's death, his glove continued to teach me about his love.

MINNESOTA MAGAZINE, SUMMER 2019

Introduction

I don't have as much sports memorabilia in my office as you might expect. A Bauer hockey stick signed by members of the 2000–01 Bloomington Jefferson High School hockey team I wrote about in *Blades of Glory*. A Max baseball bat signed by Rod Carew from a Twins fantasy camp. A pint-sized football signed by Fran Tarkenton that a radio host gave me in appreciation for appearing on his show. And a Wilson baseball glove that belonged to my dad.

Shortly before he died, my dad gave me his baseball glove. It's one of those big leather blobs with thick fingers, a Wilson model maybe 70 years old. On the band of leather that wrapped around his wrist, my dad had etched his name, BILL ROSENGREN. All caps. The "B" and "R" have the flourish of his creative side (the former *Minnesota Daily* cartoonist); the other letters display his impeccable penmanship (the dutiful law student). He used a wood burning tool, whose mark would endure longer than a pen's ink. The glove, worn and aged, has preserved his personality.

I imagine the glove new: dark brown, aromatic leather. My dad, 13, 14 years old, tenderly rubbing oil into the pocket. I picture that boy—the skinny kid with short blond hair I know from black-and-white photographs—scooping groundballs with that lumpy glove, clapping his free hand over the pocket to trap the ball.

He played in a park near Minnehaha Falls. A road has since erased the field, but his stories about the games linger. My favorite is of the kid who slugged a ball that crashed into the popcorn cart past left field, breaking glass and scattering players—except for the batter, who gleefully rounded the bases before fleeing the popcorn vendor.

In another photograph, this one from the early 1950s, my dad poses with his navy shipmates in baseball uniforms, the glove resting on his knee. He played second base in a tournament against Alaskan teams during his ship's tour. I hardly recognize the young man—front row, second from the left—with several days' growth of beard. As my father, he was always clean shaven. I marvel that he had lived almost half of his life before I knew him.

Pondering that glove today, I'm curious about the time he bought it, probably with money from his paper route. Was he one of the first among his buddies to have a glove? One of the last? When someone dies, things we never thought to ask assume a sudden importance and stoke in us a desire to know, as though that knowing would bring the lost one closer to us, would ease the separation brought by death, soften its permanence.

This ache to know our parents often visits us too late. Yet had it come earlier for me, I'm not sure it would have been satisfied. My dad was a difficult man to get to know, a Swede who could go long stretches without speaking. Born in 1934, he was native to a generation of men who did not discuss their emotions. He shared some memories but not about his father who disappeared on drinking binges; not about his mother, bitter about working to pay her husband's gambling debts. So often, that's the way it is. We're left with a view from the outside wishing we could know what it was like inside.

*   *   *

Today, I pick the glove off the shelf and slide my hand into it. Part of the beauty of an old leather glove is the way it shapes to one's hand, formed by so many days of sunshine and sweat. The glove does not fit me the way it did my dad. It's stiff in places, short in the fingers, wide in the palm.

I'm surprised to feel deep inside the fingers the leather has broken open and the ragged edges chafe my skin. The exposed padding is soft, tender. It seems I have stumbled upon a secret, something intimate I had not known. Maybe my dad knew I would, and this was his way of letting me glimpse what it had been like to be him.

Postscript

After this essay appeared in the University of Minnesota alumni magazine, a sports broadcaster for a local television station taped a segment about me and my dad's glove for the evening news. The essay and news segment prompted several people to contact me to tell me the stories of their fathers' old gloves. My favorite was from the guy whose father, a lieutenant on a World War II tank landing ship, had lent his first baseman's mitt to one of his men for a pickup game when they stopped at Bikini Atoll in 1945. Fifty years later, the man returned the glove to the son.

FIELD OF DREAMS

Some guys buy a sports car, have an affair, or get a tattoo in midlife crisis. I did something crazier—returned to the scene of my wayward youth—and emerged redeemed.

SPIRITUALITY & HEALTH, JULY/AUGUST 2015

Introduction

If you could have a do-over, what would you do? For me, it meant suiting up again.

A singular regret has dogged me into middle age: the way I betrayed baseball. I loved the game—played it whenever I could, collected boxfuls of cards, delighted in watching the Twins, memorized their batting averages. At 16, I was a starting outfielder for my high school jayvee team. Until the day a buddy told me he had a bag of pot, and I skipped practice to get stoned with him. I didn't know how to excuse my absence to the coach the next day, so I skipped practice and got stoned again. The day after that I simply turned in my uniform. My blooming drug addiction had been engulfing my life; baseball became its latest casualty.

I sobered up senior year, played some softball in college, married, and started raising kids. One constant—in addition to my sobriety—remained my love of baseball. I devoured books and articles on the subject, continued to follow the Twins, made pilgrimages to famous ballparks, and wrote countless articles and three books of my own about this great game.

Back on the field coaching my son's Little League team, the thwack of the ball in my glove, the dust kicked up in the infield, and the weight of a bat in my hands reminded me how much I had enjoyed playing myself. I couldn't help but wonder what if I had not skipped practice that fateful afternoon—would I still ache to play again?

I mentioned this to a guy at my 12-step meeting who played in a 35-over league. Next day, a friend of his who managed another team in the league called. Which is how I wound up in left field on a cloudless Wednesday evening in June. Two months shy of my 48th birthday, I hadn't played competitive baseball in 31 years. But I didn't want to pass up the chance to reverse a wayward decision—nay, impulse—of my youth.

I was still fit, but on my way to the park I had worried that I might be on my way to humiliation. Once there, I introduced myself to the other guys and discovered that several were new as well, including a Jim Leyland doppelganger who could still snap a curveball, and Adam, a pigeon-toed shortstop who had answered a newspaper ad. Turned out half a dozen guys from last year's Rockets had defected to other teams, and the regulars were just happy to have a full roster.

The manager gave me a maroon jersey with a big *R* on the chest and a pair of white pants. When I put on the uniform along with my old spikes, I was suddenly 10 years old all over, pretending to be Harmon Killebrew. Jogging out to left field, I couldn't believe I was getting the chance to play baseball again after so many years.

The game was harder to play than I remembered. In the first inning, I started back on a line drive but not nearly fast enough, and the ball soared over my head all the way to the the 340-foot sign. Two foul balls sailed out of my reach, though I could have gotten to the second one in high school. In the third inning I took off for a shot to left-center. I seemed to have it lined up correctly. *I can catch this,* I thought excitedly and shoved my glove high to snag the drive—but felt only emptiness. The ball whizzed past. Damnit. I cut sharply to give chase, and my right glute protested. I got the ball back to the infield—at least I hit the cutoff man—but the pain in my buttocks reminded me I was no longer a teenager.

Batting proved even more difficult. The first pitch that screamed past—Strike!—let me know this was leagues different from the tennis balls my 10-year-old threw me in the front yard. I popped up meekly in front of the plate.

In the bottom half of the final frame, I batted with two on, one out. I didn't want to mess up in the midst of our last-chance rally. The count mounted to 3–2. *Okay,* I told myself like I told the kids I coached, *protect the plate.* I choked up. The pitch missed wide. I eventually scored on another walk. From the dugout, I watched our third baseman, a grandfather, ground out with the bases loaded to seal our loss.

I finished the night 0-for-3 with a walk and a run scored. I handled five balls in the field, made one throwing error, and suffered a slight muscle pull that promised to be sore the next day. I counted the evening a personal victory.

How often in middle age do we get the chance for a do-over on a regret from our youth? I carried home the memory of standing in the outfield grass under the blue sky, tickled by joy, and thinking, *Thank you.*

Postscript

I ended up playing four seasons with the Richfield Rockets, until a fluke injury to my throwing shoulder sustained during a hockey game ended my baseball career. Before my premature retirement, I had spent a few more games in the outfield but mostly played catcher, my preferred position. I didn't have the arm for it—I was lucky to throw out a couple of runners trying to steal second during a season—but I liked being part of the action on every pitch. My accumulated batting average over those four seasons was slightly above the Mendoza Line. As time passes, I don't get any better in my mind; the memories of the way the game humbled me remain fresh. So do the memories of the good times on and off the field with my teammates playing a game I still love. I'm deeply grateful to Ron Cottone, the Rockets' manager, for giving me the chance to cultivate those memories—and simply to play again.

WALTER MITTY MEETS BERT BLYLEVEN

What happens when a middle-aged guy attempts to revive his high school baseball career at a fantasy camp?

NINE JOURNAL, SPRING 2021

Introduction

Nobody fantasizes about being mediocre. In our daydreams, we pitch the perfect game in the World Series like Don Larsen or come off the bench to hit the walk-off home run like Kirk Gibson. But fantasy camp has a way of correcting illusions about our abilities.

Genesis: In the Big Inning

"I want to pitch from that mound," my buddy Tom Knickelbine said. He pointed from our seats along the third-base line at Target Field to where Glen Perkins stood. "Guys who attend fantasy camp get to play a game here next summer."

"You're going to fantasy camp?"

"Yeah." TK had pitched in high school, taken 30 years off to go to college, finish med school, get married, and have three children, but resumed his career last summer on our 35-over baseball team. "You should come, too."

Sounded fun, but I knew my wife would never go for me leaving her alone with our two young kids for a week. And I couldn't justify writing a check for $4,195. Besides, much as I loved the game, I didn't want to become some Walter Mitty parody. "Nah."

I thought that was it until a couple of months later when TK sent an email telling me he'd registered and told the camp director about his writer friend. "Call him."

I did. The director invited me as his guest. Then my wife surprised me—she agreed to the idea. So on a January morning with temps registering 10 below in Minneapolis, I boarded the plane bound for fantasy camp in Fort Myers, Florida.

Enter at Your Own Risk

The sign on the door at the Player Development Complex read: "RE-STRICTED AREA: Staff, players, and coaches only!!!!" Like every other one of the 132 campers there (including four women), TK and I had not gained access with our talents but could now enter the previously forbidden sphere. We opened the door and walked into the clubhouse.

My locker was larger than any I'd ever had: a wooden cubicle three feet wide with a nameplate above it and a metal folding chair tucked inside. There were two Twins jerseys—home and away—the blue one with my name across the back above No. 13. I had been too self-conscious to pick the number of my boyhood hero, Rod Carew, so I had chosen that of John Roseboro, a fellow catcher who had played two seasons with the Twins and was the subject of my latest book. There was also a Max bat with my name engraved on it.

The camp format had us divided into 10 teams, each coached by a pair of pros. TK and I played for Greg Gagne, shortstop on the Twins' two World champion teams, and Frank Viola, the ace of the 1987 team. I had met Viola at the camp dinner the night before. He's a big guy, 6-foot-4 and heavier than the 200 pounds he played at—all of these pros are bigger in real life than they appeared on television and the field. Viola sported a hoodie, red curly mop, thick mustache, and New York accent. Despite the diamond-studded No. 16 hanging from a thin gold chain around his neck, he seemed more a happy-go-lucky galumph than a three-time All-Star and the 1988 Cy Young Award winner. "Good to meet you," Sweet Music said, like it had been on his bucket list. "I hope you have some fun."

Still, my first at-bat, I felt the nerves. I wanted to prove I wasn't a total imposter in my Twins uniform. The guy on the mound was throwing about the speed of the pitchers I had faced in my summer league since resuscitating my high school baseball career two years ago, but I have never been confident about my hitting. It didn't calm me to hear Viola yell from the first-base coach's box, "Okay, John, make a good debut."

I flied out to right-center. But at least I didn't embarrass myself during the game—beyond bouncing a throw past the third baseman when starting the ball around the horn following a strikeout. I blocked plenty of balls in the dirt, though when I told Viola I was frustrated I'd gone 0-for-4, he ribbed me: "Hey, it can't get any worse."

All in the Family

The majority of the campers came from Minnesota, this being a Twins camp after all and held in Florida during January, but others drifted in from as far away as San Francisco and Montreal. Doctors, attorneys, math teachers, software developers, mechanics, engineers, cops, even a Catholic priest came looking to indulge their baseball jones by playing games and mingling with former pros. Many of them had been there before, multiple times. The ages spread from Curt Sampson, just the other side of 80, to his 20-year-old grandson. (The elder Sampson actually pitched a complete-game victory, allowing only one run.) Campers needed to be at least 30 years old unless they signed up with a family member. There were 14 pairs of father-sons, two pairs of father-daughters. There was the multigenerational Sampson clan, Jim Duval with his four sons, and Mark Hodge with his three boys. Mark had been coming to camp for five years; this year he paid the freight for Chris, 37; Rob, 36; and Jake, 27. The trip, centered around their father's love of baseball, replaced their past fishing excursions. "Here we all get to be twelve years old again together," Mark said.

Frequently, the fathers formed battery combinations with their kids, reviving games of catch they'd played in the back yard. Lloyd Pallansch, whom everyone called "Papa Smurf" because of his resemblance to the bearded character, dropped the first three pitches his son threw. "I realized I was watching his face, to see how much he was enjoying himself, instead of the ball," Papa Smurf said.

Just as I fell in the median age-wise, so too did I talent-wise as a weak-hitting, soft-armed catcher who could stop a low pitch, called a good game, and could outsprint most other 49-year-olds. The talent ranged among the other campers from guys who had played college ball to one man who didn't register a hit all week. There are no scouts at fantasy camp, but we were keeping score, and I wanted to play my best, or maybe even a little better. I identified with one guy who told me, "I don't come here with any illusions about my skills. I know my limitations. But I find myself wanting to play just a little better than I can, and when I don't, that frustrates me."

The Beginning of a Beautiful Friendship

Every camp has its character; ours had two: Bert Blyleven and Derrick Doescher.

Blyleven, a Hall of Famer as renowned for his practical jokes as his curveball, currently puts the color into Twins' television broadcasts and served as judge of the kangaroo court. "The rules of the court are that there are no rules," he said.

Doescher, a 27-year-old grease monkey from Mankato, sported the only Mohawk in camp, which sprouted five inches high. He animated the field with his loud proclamations of "GREAAAAAAT pupils!" and the like.

One night in the bar, he suddenly blurted, "Hey, I'm drinking with the wrong hand." He claimed he had ordered beer only to ice the palm of his catching hand. Apparently he had taken so much treatment he'd forgotten the procedure.

The honorary Blyleven, presiding in a mop wig and black robes, seized upon Derrick's unorthodox locks in the court's first session. Blyleven fined him $14, one dollar for each spike he counted. "But how could you count that high?" Derrick retorted. "You didn't take off your shoes."

The two became fast buddies. They traded wisecracks, and Blyleven chauffeured Derrick in his Hummer from the field to the hotel. At the end of the week, in the court's second session, Blyleven wore a faux Mohawk himself with his robes. "The court recognized the other night that we are a new generation, and we have decided to come down to your level," he proclaimed.

Funny Thing Happened on the Way to the Ballpark

Humor spiced the camp. TK had some control issues his first game and plunked all three Hodge boys. "The only one of us you didn't get was our old man," one son said. So Mark Hodge approached TK in the clubhouse afterward, handed him a ball, took several steps back, flinched, and said, "Okay, I'm ready."

My teammate Chris Shinkle came back to the dugout after grounding out to the shortstop. "I want my money back," he said. "My fantasy was to put it in those trees."

On the day after the BBWAA members' Hall of Fame vote, a camper asked a panel of the pros if they thought Pete Rose should be inducted. "Well," former Twins outfielder Mickey Hatcher said with mock disgust, "he did give me a bad tip on a horse that finished last. . . ."

After one of his players lined a base hit to right field, Juan Berenguer, former Twins pitcher turned first-base coach, called to the right fielder, "Hey, that's his first fantasy camp hit. Can I have the ball to give him?" When the fielder tossed Berenguer the ball, the coach sent his batter to second base.

Everybody Loves a Bargain

There was an easy rapport between the former pros and current campers, facilitated by the humor and time spent together in the clubhouse, on the fields, and at meals. One morning, I sat down for breakfast with Berenguer, notorious for intimidating batters by scowling and throwing inside. Señor Smoke proved a nice guy, smiling benignly and telling me the story of being in Managua as a 17-year-old for a baseball tournament with the Panamanian national team in late December 1972. "Twenty minutes after our plane took off, they told us an earthquake had flattened our hotel," he said. Roberto Clemente died on his way to aid victims of that earthquake. "My mother used to tell me life could change just like that."

At lunch one day, Tony Oliva, the great left-handed hitter whom I remembered vividly from his knock-kneed stance after several knee injuries, told me the story of coming to the United States as a teenage prospect from Cuba without knowing a word of English. "Someone wrote on a piece of paper for me 'ham and eggs' and 'fried chicken,'" he said. "That's all I ate for months."

I ran into Gagne toting a shopping bag in the hotel stairwell. He had saved 30 percent on the shirts and pants he bought by signing up for one of the store's credit cards. "I saved $130," he said happily. Hearing this from a guy who made over $20 million playing professional baseball, I realized we were more alike than different—he just had a much better arm, which provided a more lucrative career path.

Excuse Me, Aren't You . . .

But I was still apprehensive about approaching my boyhood hero when Rod Carew showed up in our dugout. Here was the Twins' seven-time batting champion whose unusual stance we all used to imitate, now standing five feet from me. Do I tell him I'm a writer? No, that might put him on the defensive; he never liked the press. Do I say, "I used to pretend I was you?" No, that might creep him out. So I just waited and tried not to stare like an idiot.

Serendipitously, he asked, "What's the score?"

"Three to one, us," I said. "See that woman playing second? She was up with the score tied 1–1, bases loaded, two outs, two strikes, and she blooped a single to right—much like Rod Carew would have done."

He smiled. This was going well.

"Drove in two runs. When the next batter asked for some Quick Dry to be spread in the batter's box where the dirt was mushy, she told Viola coaching first, 'That's where I shit my pants.'"

That cracked up Carew. I survived that critical first impression.

Everyday Hero

They say you shouldn't meet your heroes. Few men can measure up to the illusions we've created of them, but Carew withstood the test.

At dinner I had the chance to chat casually with him, asking if it was true he used to practice his bunting by laying down a towel as a target during BP ("Yes, a face towel."), about learning to steal home ("[Twins manager] Billy Martin knew we would have some close games and wanted me to be able to do that to help win them."), and whether he was safe an eighth time in 1969, which would have broken Ty Cobb's record for most times stealing home in a single season ("Yes, the catcher dropped the ball between his legs, but the ump stumbled and wasn't in position to see it.").

Finally, I asked him if it was weird having middle-aged men wearing jerseys with his number. "When I see them smile, the way their faces light up, I feel good that I can do that for him," he said thoughtfully. "Isn't that what it's all about, being able to spread joy?"

After dinner Carew presented Mark Haigh, a camper with leukemia in remission, an autographed jersey. Carew lost his youngest daughter to leukemia in 1996 when she was only 18. That inspired his cause to raise awareness and money for cancer research, which has given guys like Mark Haigh a far better chance of survival. The two had met the day before, when Haigh waited in the corner for the long line of guys wanting Carew's autograph to clear then told Carew his story. The father who had buried his daughter spoke to the younger man with compassion and encouragement. "When I walked out of there with tears in my eyes, I realized that Rod Carew the baseball player had been my childhood hero," Mark told us. "I found out yesterday Rod Carew the man is my real-life hero."

Just Rub Some Dirt on It

The injuries mounted as the week wore on. None of us were used to playing two seven-inning games daily. One guy had to fly home early for emergency surgery on his biceps tendon. Mark Hodge's oldest son Chris hobbled around on crutches after messing up his knee. Bill Clabots, a restaurant owner in the Twin Cities, showed me in the bar one evening where six foul tips had struck him, all avoiding his equipment. His wife Connie had shown up only to find Bill sprawled on the ground after a ball caught him in the throat. She sat down in the bleachers. "Weren't you worried?" I asked.

"No," she replied. "Bill's been beaten up a lot playing ball. That's his thing."

What Would Bert Do?

The line lengthened daily in the training room, where three trainers rubbed, stretched, and applied ice packs. A massage therapist worked overtime. Ibuprofen and beer became the PEDs of choice.

My throwing shoulder ached a bit (probably from rifling a throw into center field on a play at second base), but my knees and legs had borne the strain of catching and running without complaint. TK wasn't so lucky.

He already wore a brace after corrective surgery on his left knee, but in his first game pitching he tweaked the medial meniscus of his right knee. He further aggravated it in the second game he pitched, a one-run gem. "It's fun watching the two of you work together," Viola told us afterward, which we both appreciated.

Friday morning, we had our first playoff game. Win and we played a final game for fifth place. Lose and we were done. TK was our squad's best pitcher, but Viola decided to play it safe, starting another guy who had pitched a win and hoping TK's aching knee would allow him to pitch the next day. But after our starter struggled through three innings and we trailed 4–0, TK realized this could be his last chance to pitch at camp. In a gutsy performance, he threw three solid innings, giving up only one un-earned run. However, we failed to score any runs ourselves. So our season ended, but not before TK threw a Blylevenesque curve in the final inning that buckled the batter's knees. I saw him smile despite his throbbing knee.

Reality Bites

My best play had come early in the week, before I realized that would be my only highlight moment. I chased a high foul pop down the third-base line. The ball seemed within my range, but the wind swatted it around. I managed to snag the ball across my body in front of the opposing dugout. The next day in the clubhouse, Lee Stange, former Twins pitcher who had been coaching the other team, teased me about being too old to play catcher but then complimented me on my catch. I tucked that into my bag of souvenirs.

Throughout the week, I managed a couple of walks, a base hit that drove in two runs and, during the pro-rookie game, a single off Rick Aguilera. The closer for the 1991 Twins grooved me a meatball, but ulti-mately I felt discouraged by my hitting—or lack of it. I had struck out twice looking and tapped several soft balls up the middle. Getting on base because of errors or outrunning a possible double-play ball offered no consolation. Reality trumped my fantasy.

Look at How the Fish Live

The pros kept telling me they were having fun. I've digested a lot of clichés from athletes, but this one seemed sincere. They had the chance to recon-nect with old teammates. They joked with the campers. They told stories about the glory days, reliving their past, which allowed them to become ballplayers once again, even if it was only in their memories. "It's fun for us, seeing you guys, some who haven't played for 25 to 30 years, having fun playing baseball," Viola said. "You get to see how we lived."

That's probably the biggest boon for campers: fantasy camp conjures dreams of the future they never had. They get to live the life of a pro ball-player, playing games, rehashing them, hanging in the clubhouse. They get to meet boyhood heroes, kick back with former pros, hear entertaining sto-ries. It's expensive, costing thousands of dollars and, in some cases, physical injury. And, of course, it exposes the folly of our dreams, sending us home with the realization that we are has-beens who never were.

Say Goodbye to Mr. Roarke

Sunday morning, we dispersed. On the flight headed back to Minneapolis, I spotted John Duvall, whom I'd played against in our last game and sat next to at dinner the last night. "Hey, aren't you that ballplayer?"

"No."

"I guess that's one question the camp answered," I said.

With our uniforms tucked into our suitcases, he was once again a financial advisor, I a writer, and TK a cardiologist. But we also toted the memories of an extraordinary week. I realized Viola was right. He had told us before our last game it wouldn't matter whether we won or lost, what we took home would be the experience. I had missed that, taking myself too seriously, but now I understood.

Plus, we still had that reunion game at Target Field to play. That would be fun.

Postscript

TK and I carpooled to the reunion game, which was very crowded—all those campers divided among only two teams. Once I finally got put in at catcher, I made a trip to the pitcher's mound. "I don't have anything to say," I told our pitcher. "I just wanted to see what the view of Target Field was like from here." I must say, it was pretty good. I'm glad TK had talked me into going to the fantasy camp and that he, too, was finally able to have the chance to enjoy the view himself.

Chapter 6

IN JACKIE'S MEMORY

THE DAY THE KLAN PLAYED BALL

In 1925 a barnstorming baseball team of African Americans took on the Ku Klux Klan team from Lodge No. 6 in Wichita, Kansas.

MEMORIES & DREAMS, OPENING DAY 2020

Introduction

When I happened upon an account of the Ku Klux Klan playing a baseball game against an all-Black team, I thought, *I've got to write about this.*

Members of the Ku Klux Klan possessed irrepressible power—their anonymity secured by hoods and their actions backed by local law enforcement—but on a Sunday afternoon during the summer of 1925, the Klan suffered defeat at the hands of a gang of African Americans armed with baseball bats. And gloves.

The beating occurred on a baseball diamond, Island Park to be specific, in Wichita, Kansas, on June 21, 1925, when the all-Black Wichita Monrovians, a barnstorming team, played a game against the KKK nine of Lodge No. 6.

The Wichita Monrovians—who had played two previous seasons independently as the Black Wonders—joined eight other teams from Oklahoma, Nebraska, and Kansas in 1922 to form the Colored Western League. The Monrovians took their name from the capital of Liberia, founded in part by former slaves who had known the Klan's terror. Team alumni included catcher T. J. Young, pitcher Nelson Dean, and third baseman Newt Joseph—all of whom eventually played for the Kansas City Monarchs, though none of them participated in the Monrovians' 1925 game against the Klan.

The Monrovians won the pennant in the Colored Western League's debut season, but that would be its only season. The league, troubled by financial challenges and infighting among team leaders, folded after one year.

The Monrovians survived. The team was owned and operated by the Monrovian Corporation, whose capital stock was valued at $10,000. Run by a collection of Black businessmen, it was a healthy enterprise. The Monrovians owned their ballpark in the heart of Wichita's Black neighborhood, which put them in charge of their schedule and in receipt of the gate without being beholden to a landlord—unheard of for ballclubs like theirs. The team became a leading philanthropic and social force in Wichita's Black community, funding organizations like the Phyllis Wheatley Children's Home.

Without a league, the Monrovians resorted to barnstorming, playing Black and white teams from Kansas and beyond. The team and its success—in 1923, it was 52–8—became a rallying point and diversion for Wichita's 6,500 African Americans, a fifth of whom lived in poverty, and all of whom lived under Jim Crow. Though Kansas had entered the Union 64 years earlier as a free state, in 1925 racial segregation still ruled. Blacks in Wichita could not order a sandwich at the Dockum Drug Store (where the first lunch counter sit-in would occur in 1958). Visiting Black players could only stay in hotels designated for "Coloreds." At the movie theater, designated Black sections preserved the best seats for white patrons.

The prevailing attitudes underlying segregation denied Wichita's African Americans—less than a tenth of the city's total population—housing in certain neighborhoods, employment opportunities, and equal education. "The Ku Klux Klan way of thinking was the way of life for a Black person in Kansas," says Phil Dixon, baseball historian and author of *The Negro Leagues: A Photographic History*.

In those times, the Monrovian ballpark at 12th and Mosley offered a sanctuary from the daily whips and scorns of discrimination. It was there "Black Wichitans [found] a place to socialize and be comfortable among other Blacks without feeling the stinging pain of racism," writes scholar Jason Pendleton in his article "Jim Crow Strikes Out."

The Ku Klux Klan contributed to the persecution. Since its revival in 1915, the organization had grown in a decade to 4 million members nationwide, with an estimated 40,000 of those in Kansas, and 6,000 in Wichita—almost one Klan member for every African American. Knights of the KKK were embedded in nearly every institution, from city governments to banks. Membership was so widespread that even Tom Baird, co-owner of the Kansas City Monarchs, joined the Klan.

The Klan saw itself as a protector of patriotic and protestant ideals threatened by immigrants, Jews, Catholics, and, of course, Blacks. The local Klavern asserted in the *Wichita Eagle* in 1922 that it "supported Jim Crow laws; the abolition of secret societies among Negroes; and no employment of Negroes under any circumstances."

Leading up to the baseball game played between the Klan and the Monrovians, there were a record number of lynchings nationwide in the first six months of 1925 (nine). "The Kansas Klan intimidated African Americans in its attempts to create a 'racially morally pure' state," Pendleton writes.

William Allen White, editor of the *Emporia Gazette*, ran for governor in 1924 on an anti-Klan platform, calling out the secret society's campaign of terror and branding its members a "body of moral idiots." White lost his bid, but sentiment against the Klan had taken root. The Kansas Supreme Court ruled in January 1925 that the Klan was a sales organization—not a charitable entity—and barred it from doing business without a charter. The state turned down the Klan's application for a charter on June 3, 1925.

The KKK, which had tried to promote itself as good for society by donating money to the local hospital and giving away food baskets to needy families, faced extinction in the state. Desperate to preserve itself, it may very well have agreed to play the all-Black Monrovian team as a public relations ploy. "On some level, it was a matter of proving superiority," says Donna Rae Pearson, a Topekan librarian who researched the game for the Kansas State Historical Society. "The Klan figured, 'We're going to beat you because we're superior beings.'"

The Monrovians certainly had their pride at stake, but their motivation was probably mostly financial. Their games against white teams always drew well, but a matchup against the Klan promised a large gate. They solicited their fans to attend the game to be played at the white ballpark on the point of Ackerman Island in the Arkansas River. "There was racial pride on the line, but also money to be made," Dixon says.

The *Wichita Beacon* announced, "Strangle holds, razors, horsewhips, and other violent implements of argument will be barred at the baseball game"—perhaps tongue in cheek, but even still, such a comment hinted at the possibility of violence in the charged atmosphere between opponents of such extremities. To keep the game under control, the teams agreed on a pair of impartial umpires: Irish Garrety and Dan Dwyer, both white and Roman Catholic.

They must have done their job because there were no reports of violence in the stands or on the field during or after the game.

A heat wave driven by scalding winds and temps topping 100 degrees could not keep away the large numbers of Blacks and whites who filled Island Park Sunday afternoon, June 21—far more than attended the other three baseball games played elsewhere that day in Wichita. The tension throughout the first half of the game soared as high as the mercury, with the score tied 1–1 through five innings.

Perhaps the heat wilted the pitchers, because the game turned into an explosion of runs, the lead going back and forth—the fate of the two teams and their fans hanging in the balance—until the Monrovians won 10–8.

The Monrovians' victory did not eradicate prejudice or eliminate segregation, but for one day at the ballpark, the Black community could exalt in finishing on top. And, in the days that followed, the Monrovians could take pride in the fact that they had done their part in ushering the Klan out of Kansas and cleansing their state of the organization's unbridled bigotry.

Postscript

Chuck Brodsky, baseball folk singer who has chronicled so many of the game's quirky moments, sums up the game in this verse from his song, "The Monrovians vs. the Klan": "It was a very good game of baseball said the newspaperman / The day the all-Black Monrovians beat the Ku Klux Klan."

ENTER ELSTON HOWARD, THE YANKEES' JACKIE ROBINSON EIGHT YEARS LATE

Why did it take America's team so long to integrate?

SPORTS ILLUSTRATED, APRIL 2015

Introduction

I had wanted to write a biography about Elston Howard, who integrated the Yankees, but my agent was not able to sell the proposal. I wrote this article instead.

April 13, 1955, was a good day for the Yankees. They kicked off their season by trouncing the Washington Senators 19–1 in the Bronx. Mickey Mantle had three hits, including a home run; Yogi Berra also homered; and Whitey Ford threw a complete game while allowing fewer hits (two) than he had himself (three, plus four RBIs). But New York's most significant player that day never got off the bench. Two days shy of eight years exactly after Jackie Robinson hurdled Major League Baseball's color barrier, Elston Howard became the first Black player to don Yankees pinstripes.

The delay by America's most popular and successful team to integrate had led to everything from editorials to picket lines, all of which had been ignored by New York's top brass. In his book *Baseball's Great Experiment*, author Jules Tygiel quotes general manager George Weiss as saying, "The Yankees are not going to promote a Negro player to the Stadium simply in order to be able to say that they have such a player. We are not going to bow to pressure groups on this issue."

To be fair, New York's roster didn't have many holes in those years, not when the team was winning six World Series titles from 1947 to 1954. But there were certainly weak links that could have been bolstered had the Yankees not been so slow to embrace integration. Howard's debut made New York the 13th of the 16 major-league franchises then in existence to employ a Black player. Weiss had previously passed on opportunities to sign Ernie Banks and Willie Mays, among others, and comments from Yankees staffers suggested prejudice had factored into keeping the team's lineup all-white.

In *Baseball's Great Experiment*, traveling secretary Bill McCorry is quoted as saying of the then-19-year-old Mays, "The kid can't hit a curveball" and, after Mays's early success with the Giants, "I got no use for him or any of them. No n----- will ever have a berth on any train I'm running."

As recalled in Roger Kahn's seminal 1972 book *The Boys of Summer*, Weiss had said in 1952 that having a Black ballplayer would draw undesirables to the Stadium. "We don't want that sort of crowd," he said. "It would offend boxholders from Westchester to have to sit with n-----s."

Money was another factor behind the Yankees' resistance to integrate. In August 1946, the team's then owner and general manager, Larry MacPhail, chaired a special committee that reported to new commissioner Happy Chandler. The report stated, in part, "the relationship of the Negro player, and/or the existing Negro Leagues to Professional Baseball is a real problem," in large part because MLB integration could cause the demise of the Negro Leagues. That, MacPhail's committee noted, would cost teams like the Yankees the nearly $100,000 it netted annually from renting the stadium to the Black Yankees, a Negro Leagues team.

Nevertheless, in late July 1953, New York seemed ready to call up Vic Power, a dark-skinned Puerto Rican who was tearing up the triple-A American Association with his hitting. Instead, Weiss surprised the press and fans by promoting Gus Triandos, a white player from Double A. "It would appear that the only advantage Triandos had was one of circumstance in not being born a Negro," Joe Bostic wrote in the *New York Amsterdam News.*

Power was a strong hitter who was on his way toward winning the American Association batting crown with a .349 average. The Yankees seemed more concerned that he dated light-skinned women, a common convention in his native Puerto Rico but one that went against American social mores of the time. Weiss traded Power to the Philadelphia Athletics that winter. "Maybe he can play, but not for us," Weiss is quoted as saying in Kahn's book, *The Era: 1947–57.* "He's impudent and he goes for white women. Power is not the Yankee type."

The next spring, New York invited a strong-armed outfielder named Elston Howard to camp, where the team surprised him with the idea of converting him into a catcher. The Yankees already had an indomitable catcher in Berra, who that season would win his second of three AL MVP Awards. Conspiracy theorists claimed this was a ploy for the team to submerge Howard in its farm system, and indeed New York assigned him to Triple A. The *Baltimore Afro-American*'s Sam Lacy characterized Howard as a "victim" and a "pawn" and quoted him complaining about his treatment. Howard denied the quote and asserted, "I ought to punch that guy's head off."

Howard made his biggest statement on the field, where he won the league MVP Award that summer, earning a promotion to the Bronx for the 1955 season. He made his major-league debut on April 14 in Boston, taking over in left field in the bottom of the sixth. He made his first and only plate appearance of the day in the eighth inning, lining a solid single to center field to score Mantle, though New York lost 8–4.

Howard didn't make his first start until April 28, when he went 3-for-5 with two runs scored and two RBIs in an 11–4 win at Kansas City. He played 97 games in all that season, finishing with a .290 average, 10 home runs, and 43 RBIs and helping the Yankees reach the World Series. He then played all seven games of the fall classic—hitting a home run in game one—but he batted just .192 and made the final out of New York's seven-game loss to the Dodgers.

In time, Howard would become a star himself. He won the 1963 American League MVP, helped the Yankees win nine pennants and four World Series, and had his No. 32 retired in 1984. But the prejudice he faced didn't cease with his promotion to the majors. His manager, Casey Stengel, is quoted in Robert Creamer's biography *Stengel* as calling Howard "n----" and "Eightball." Several of Howard's teammates, however, welcomed the rookie. Moose Skowron picked him up at the train station; Hank Bauer invited him to join other players in the hotel dining room; Berra and Phil Rizzuto socialized with him.

Perhaps the most notable sign of his acceptance came a month after his debut. On May 14, he came to bat in the bottom of the ninth inning with two outs, two runners on, and the Yankees trailing the Tigers 6–5. Howard laced a triple to left that scored Joe Collins and Mantle, giving New York a 7–6 win. When Howard reached the clubhouse, he found that Collins and Mantle had laid out an honorary carpet of white towels from his locker to the shower. He was officially one of their own.

Postscript

Howard played for the Yankees until they traded the 38-year-old midway through the 1967 season to the Red Sox. He retired after the 1968 season with a .322 lifetime batting average over 14 years. He was a 12-time All Star and two-time Gold Glove recipient. Howard became the first Black coach in the American League when the Yankees hired him to coach first base in 1969, a position he held for 10 years. (Buck O'Neil was the first Black coach in the major leagues, hired by the Chicago Cubs in 1962.)

CROSSING THE LINE

As baseball's first African American manager, Frank Robinson fulfilled Jackie Robinson's vision but failed to fully integrate the game.

HISTORY CHANNEL MAGAZINE, MAY/JUNE 2007

Introduction

Trivia question for you: Who was the first Black man to manage in the major leagues? Hint: It's not who you think. Give up? Read on for the answer.

At the 1972 World Series to commemorate the 25th anniversary of his crossing baseball's color barrier, Jackie Robinson told the crowd in Cincinnati and those watching the national television broadcast that Major League Baseball had yet to finish what he started. "I'd like to see a Black man managing the ballclub," the white-haired grandson of a slave said.

Frank Robinson was one of the millions at home watching Jackie on television. *He's right*, Frank thought. *It's past due. I hope I'll be able to see that, too, one day.*

Frank was a natural for the role. Not only had he proven himself a Hall of Fame–caliber player, he had managed five seasons in the Puerto Rican winter league. He was smart, a natural leader, and driven to win. As a boy growing up in Oakland, he had dreamed of being a pro ballplayer, not a manager, but the game had seeped into his blood. By 1962, he knew he didn't want to leave baseball and started thinking about managing. Ever outspoken, he'd publicized his intentions but received no offers.

Jackie had cracked the color barrier but not broken it. Twenty-five years after he had proven that Blacks could compete on the playing field, the game's white power brokers had not entrusted leadership of a team to a Black man. There had been qualified candidates to manage—Monte Irvin, Johnny Roseboro, and Larry Doby, among them—but the white owners and general managers hired retired Black ballplayers as hitting coaches or to minor-league posts, not to manage in the majors, not even to coach third base, which required transmitting critical signals and deciding when to send runners home. The prevailing prejudice barred African Americans from positions that called for thinking, decision-making, and leadership.

Frank didn't know when he watched Jackie's speech that in two years, he would be the one to fulfill Jackie's dream, becoming the first African American hired to manage a major-league ballclub. He expected pressure in that role, but he did not realize that in furthering the integration of baseball, he would face skepticism, opposition, obstacles, hatred, and prejudice similar to what his predecessor had endured.

*   *   *

On October 3, 1974, Cleveland general manager Phil Seghi announced that he had hired Frank Robinson to manage the Indians for the 1975 season. The three television networks covered the press conference along with 100 reporters from across the country. Baseball commissioner Bowie Kuhn and American League president Lee MacPhail—neither of whom had ever attended the announcement of a manager hiring in those roles— were there. President Gerald Ford sent a congratulatory telegram. It was a historic event, but Kuhn, who had stood with Jackie at the 1972 Series, put the moment in perspective: "Now that it has happened, I'm not going to get up and shout that this is something for baseball to be exceptionally proud of, because it is so long overdue."

As a historical footnote, Frank was not the first Black man to manage in the majors. That was Ernie Banks, a coach with the Cubs in 1973, who managed the last several innings of a game when manager Whitey Lockman was ejected. Frank was the first hired. "What's really extraordinary is how long it took and, on a certain level, that it should be significant for what should have been a routine progression after Jackie broke in," says Jules Tygiel, professor of history at San Francisco State University and one of the nation's foremost authorities on race in baseball. "The major leagues weren't ready for that step."

Although the Jim Crow laws that Frank faced when he broke into the majors in 1956 were no longer practiced, their sentiment had not been erased from many Americans' minds, including those of baseball's owners and executives. "It's the same old story," Frank writes in his 1968 autobiography *My Life Is Baseball*: "The owners are just afraid. They are a step behind the public."

Baseball's white brass feared that the players, many of them from the South, where slavery had carved a permanent divide between Blacks and whites, would not follow the direction of an African American. They feared that a Black manager would upset the Black-and-white balance in the clubhouse. They feared that the fans might not support the decision. They feared the uproar that would result when—as they often had to do with managers—they fired a Black manager. Moreover, as Al Campanis, then the Dodgers' general manager, let slip in his now infamous 1987 *Nightline* interview, they feared that African Americans "lacked the necessities" to manage. Never mind the dreams of African Americans like Martin Luther King Jr. and Jackie Robinson; it was safest to stick with the status quo.

It took guts for Seghi and Indians owner Ted Bonda to hire Frank. They faced a century of thinking whose sediment seemed to have calcified in many minds.

*   *   *

Opening Day, April 8, 1975, broke cold in Cleveland. The wind hustled over Lake Erie and chilled Municipal Stadium. Frank wore a jacket before the game. Some players donned stocking caps. But it didn't keep the fans away. An announced crowd of 56,715 packed the stadium to see Frank Robinson make his managerial debut.

When the public address boomed his introduction: "the new manager of the Indians, Frank Robinson," the fans thundered their approval. Frank jogged onto the field and soaked it up. He had received many ovations over the years, but this was the "biggest and best" of his career.

Rachel Robinson, Jackie's widow, threw out the ceremonial first pitch and said she was "heartened by this symbol of progress."

The crowd cheered again when Frank, batting second as the designated hitter, came to bat in the bottom of the first inning. He slugged a 2–2 pitch over the left-field fence—the 575th home run of his career. The Cleveland fans went crazy. After the game, when Frank had notched his first managerial win, he told the reporters that crowded his office, "Right now, I feel better than I have after anything I've ever done in this game."

It would stand as the high point of a trying year. Frank not only had to prove himself as a rookie manager, he had to prove his race worthy of the challenge. He had not erased in a day the sentiment that had delayed the hiring of a Black manager for 27 years. He felt the pressure to make good on the Indians' experiment for those who would follow his lead.

Frank faced opposition from players, who second-guessed his disciplinary style and strategic decisions. Gaylord Perry, a white Southerner and 21-game winner for the Indians in 1974, had criticized the new manager's conditioning program in spring training. "I'm nobody's slave," he snapped. Several times, he complained to the press, "The way this place is run is really chickenshit."

Frank had tried unsuccessfully to clear the air in a private meeting with Perry, but later Seghi, the general manager, became involved, and even Kuhn ventured his opinion on the much-publicized dispute. Gaylord's brother Jim, another starting pitcher with the Indians that season, also voiced his exasperation with Frank's decisions.

Frank also butted heads with the disgruntled pitcher John "Blue Moon" Odom, traded to the Indians in May and dealt away three weeks later, but Odom was Black, and the press made more of Frank's conflict with catcher John Ellis, who was white. In mid-July, Frank sent up a pinch-hitter for Ellis, who flung his mask in anger, almost striking Robinson. Frank, who had already fined Ellis twice for missing hitting signals, got in his face in the dugout and, later in a private meeting, benched him.

A newspaper story suggested that race was the underlying factor in the dispute. Cleveland fans phoned the Indians' switchboard to support Ellis and to lobby for Robinson's dismissal. Letters to editors of the two Cleveland dailies supported Ellis and criticized Robinson. Seghi stood by Robinson, but it was clear that if lines were to be drawn over race in Cleveland, the Black man would fall on the short side.

Robinson faced opposition around the country as well. Bigots littered his mailbox with hate mail, and at least two issued death threats that season. One called the Indians' switchboard in June and told the operator, "If that n----- shows up tonight, we're going to kill him."

Robinson didn't stay away from the ballpark that night, but he couldn't dismiss his suspicion that racism tainted the calls of white umpires. Earlier in his playing career, Frank had received a letter from Jackie urging him to speak out on civil rights issues. As a manager, Frank confronted the issue closest at hand. He argued with the umps and baited them in the press. In one argument with ump Bill Haller, Frank pointed to the color of his arm and asked, "Does this bother you?" He shoved Jerry Neudecker after he claimed the first-base umpire bumped him in a toe-to-toe argument. American League president MacPhail suspended Robinson three games and fined him $250, though he did listen to his appeal. By the All-Star break, umpires had ejected Frank three times.

After his third ejection of the season—for telling plate umpire Larry Barnett to "punch a hole in your mask!" so he could call strikes properly— Frank accused certain umpires of prejudice against the Indians. He didn't think Barnett would've ejected a white manager for the same comment. "Certain umpires are getting back at me through my club," Robinson said. "Every close call goes against us, and I think they are taking out on the club the way they feel about me."

Twice, Robinson was tempted to quit. The first time was in mid-June, when his team was playing poorly, losing eight of nine games in one stretch, and the Cleveland fans booed everybody in an Indian uniform, including Frank. The second was in July, after his third ejection, and he was feeling paranoid about the umpires' calls. Both times, he considered resigning as manager. "Those were the worst times for me," he said. "I was very depressed, even if I didn't show it."

But Frank was not a quitter. Nor would he let his team go belly up. Even as the season wore on and the Indians floundered far south of first place, he urged his players to play their best and salvage the season. By the end of September, he had made believers out of them. Their attitude had improved, they were playing together, and the club won 27 of its last 42 games. Frank had also won the respect of managers and general managers, who praised him for pulling his team together and getting the most out of a young squad. Most importantly, he'd validated the confidence of Seghi, who renewed his contract for the 1976 season.

* * *

At the close of the 2006 season, the Washington Nationals fired Frank Robinson, ending the 71-year-old's managing career. Over parts of 17 seasons with the Indians, Giants, Orioles, Expos, and Nationals, he amassed a 1065–1176 record, mostly with undertalented teams. He had proven himself capable, but his debut had not become the watershed moment that Rachel Robinson had wished for on Opening Day 1975 when she said, "I hope this is the beginning of a lot more Black players being moved into front office and managerial positions and not just having their talents exploited on the field."

Frank furthered Jackie's legacy, but he didn't finish it. In the 32 years since Frank's managerial debut, there have been 317 manager positions filled in MLB. Only 17 have been filled by 11 African Americans (not counting Hispanics with dark skin who identify as Latino). On Opening Day 2007, there are only two Black managers among MLB's 30 teams: the New York Mets' Willie Randolph and the Texas Rangers' newly hired Ron Washington. Since the game's inception, there have been only three African American general managers. Sixty years after Jackie first crossed the color line, Major League Baseball still has not fully integrated itself.

Frank has taken up Jackie's voice. "If management were judging an individual by his qualities rather than the color of his skin, there would be more of us in those positions," Frank said. "I'd like to see better representation in baseball than there is right now."

Postscript

Since this article was published in 2007, there have been only five more Black men to manage in the major leagues. In 2020, Dave Roberts, manager of the Los Angeles Dodgers, became the second Black man to lead his team to a World Series championship. In 1992, Cito Gaston was the first with the Toronto Blue Jays.

PIONEERS OF THE NEGRO LEAGUES

How Toni Stone, Connie Morgan, and Mamie Johnson busted down the walls confining women and opened eyes.

MEMORIES & DREAMS, SPRING 2017

Introduction

My daughter Alison introduced me to Toni Stone with her seventh-grade history day project. I was pleased to see Alison's interest in a pioneering woman, especially one who played baseball. And happy to learn that Stone grew up in the Twin Cities, like my daughter, a fine athlete in her own right.

After Jackie Robinson led the exodus of talent out of the Negro Leagues and into the majors—and the fans followed—Syd Pollack, owner of the Indianapolis Clowns, was desperate to resuscitate interest in his team. The Negro National League had folded in 1948, and by 1953 the Clowns were one of only four teams left in the Negro American League. Pollack, whose promotional hijinks had earned the Clowns a designation as "the Harlem Globetrotters of baseball," had tried dressing King Tut in a tuxedo and employing a daffy dwarf as sideline entertainers. In the 1950s, he signed three women who had the talent to be more than simply gate attractions— though they accomplished that as well.

The first was Toni Stone, whom Pollack signed in 1953 to replace Hank Aaron at second base. Stone had played hardball with boys since she was a young girl. Born July 17, 1921, in West Virginia, Stone moved to St. Paul when she was 10 years old. A priest encouraged the tomboy with the strong right arm to try out for the St. Peter Claver boys team. By 16, she was pitching for a semipro team, the Twin Cities Colored Giants. She played with two more semipro teams, the San Francisco Sea Lions and the New Orleans Creoles, before agreeing to play second base for the Clowns and become the first woman to play in the Negro American League.

The fans did turn out, and some rooted for Stone's success, but in the convention-bound 1950s, not all of them were ready to embrace the idea of a woman playing on a men's team. They yelled at her from the stands, "Why don't you go home and fix your husband some biscuits?"

Her husband, Aurelious Alberga, whom she had married in 1950, would have preferred that, but Stone was headstrong and determined to prove herself. Pollack wanted her to wear a skirt like the players in the All-American Girls Professional League. She said no.

Much as Jackie Robinson's white teammates in Brooklyn weren't all ready to have a teammate of a different color, not all of Stone's Indianapolis teammates accepted her as an equal. Some made passes at her, which she quickly rebuffed. Others tried to sabotage her play by throwing the ball to her at second base in such a way that it positioned her in the path of incoming spikes.

Playing on a men's team presented challenges off the field as well. Stone had to change in the room used by the umpires. On road trips, she often stayed at brothels, a practice that began when the proprietor of the hotel where the team stayed figured she must be a prostitute when he saw her get off the bus with 28 men and gave her directions to the nearest brothel. Stone, who could identify with the brothel workers as an outsider, was welcomed by them.

Stone did not play as often as she would have liked—only about 50 of the 175 games the Clowns played in 1953 (Negro League statistics are not as plentiful or reliable as white Organized Baseball records). After the season, Pollack sold her contract to the Kansas City Monarchs, whom Stone played with in 1954 before retiring. During her two years in the Negro American League, she had a career batting average estimated to be .243, but at one point in the 1954 season she was batting .364, fourth in the league, right behind Ernie Banks.

Legend has it she rapped a single off Satchel Paige, but the archives don't corroborate the story. Still, the persistence of those who believe the story—including Martha Ackerman, author of the Stone biography *Curveball*—bears testament to Stone's skills, making such a feat plausible.

Pollack signed the 19-year-old Connie Morgan to replace Stone. The athletic Morgan had already played five seasons with the women's North Philadelphia Honey Drippers from her hometown (batting .338 over that period) and basketball for the Rockettes. When she read an article in the newspaper about Stone playing for the Clowns, Morgan wrote Pollack to request a tryout.

Oscar Charleston, the Clowns' manager (and a Hall of Fame center fielder), had scouted Morgan and called her "one of the most sensational" female players he had ever seen. Perhaps upon his recommendation, Pollack granted Morgan's request when the Clowns played an exhibition in Baltimore against the Orioles. Impressed, he signed Morgan, who had been primarily a catcher for the Honey Drippers, to play second base.

She encountered many of the gender stereotypes that Stone had. The *Baltimore Afro-American* ran a photo of Morgan in her uniform alongside another of her wearing a white dress and gloves with the caption: "Miss Connie Morgan: The baseball player and the lady." (The previous year, *Ebony* had published similar photos of Stone, one in her uniform, the other in a dress: "Dressed in street clothes, Toni Stone is an attractive young lady who could be someone's secretary, but once in uniform she is all ball player.")

Yet the *Afro-American* also recognized Morgan's unqualified baseball ability. In an account of a May game, it described how Morgan "electrified over 6,000 fans . . . when she went far to her right to make a sensational stop, flipped to shortstop Bill Holder and started a lightning double play against the Birmingham Barons."

The *New York Amsterdam News* validated the talents and temperament of Stone, Morgan, and Mamie Johnson (whom Pollack also signed in 1954) when the Clowns played the Monarchs in a doubleheader at Yankee Stadium: "The girls take a back seat to no one on the field."

Morgan played just one season in the Negro American League, splitting time at second base with Ray Neiland, batting third, and posting about a .300 average.

While Stone broke the gender barrier all alone, Morgan had the support of a female teammate in Mamie Johnson, whom Pollack also signed prior to the 1954 season. Some accounts have Johnson barnstorming with the team in late 1953. A pitcher with a slider, circle change, screwball, and a curveball she claimed to have learned from Paige, she did not throw hard but she had good control.

They called the 5-foot-3 or maybe 5-foot-2 Johnson "Peanut." Story has it that in her first game pitching for the Clowns, Hank Baylis peered from the batter's box to the diminutive pitcher on the mound and called, "What makes you think you can strike a batter out? Why, you aren't any larger than a peanut!" She struck him out, and the nickname stuck.

Good story, but newspaper accounts of her signing with the Clowns identify her already as Mamie "Peanut" Johnson. Like Morgan, she was a good all-around athlete born in South Carolina who reportedly was the first girl at her Long Branch High School (New Jersey) to play football, basketball, and baseball. In 1953, the 18-year-old Johnson went to Washington for a tryout with the All-American Girls Professional Baseball League.

She and her friend, also Black, hadn't realized that the AAGPBL remained all-white. After being ignored for 15 minutes, Johnson turned to her friend and said, "We better go. I don't think we're wanted here."

Johnson found a men's semipro team that did want her, which is where a scout for the Clowns saw her and recommended her to Pollack. The men were skeptical at first about this pint-sized pitcher, but she earned their respect with her talent. "After you prove yourself as to what you came there for, then you don't have any problem out of them, either," she said in a 2003 interview with National Public Radio.

Johnson played into 1955 with the team but left before finishing the season, saying she wanted to spend more time with her young son. By her own account, Johnson went 33–8 during her time with the Clowns, though Negro League historians question the validity of that record (again, the record books are incomplete on the subject).

Not disputed, though, is the fact that she was the first female pitcher in professional baseball and one of three courageous women to play in the Negro American League.

Though Stone, Morgan, and Johnson faced resistance during their playing days, the years have been kind to their memory. Stone was inducted into the International Women's Sports Hall of Fame in 1985, and St. Paul named a city baseball field after her. Morgan was inducted into the Pennsylvania Sports Hall of Fame in 1995. In a ceremonial MLB draft of living Negro League players in 2008, Johnson was selected by the Washington Nationals. Long after they retired, these women, who challenged the way society viewed their gender, have finally earned the respect they deserved.

Postscript

My 35-over baseball team, the Richfield Rockets, played several games in St. Paul at Toni Stone field. Knowing more of her story by then, I felt honored to play there.

Chapter 7

THE WORLD SERIES

KIRBY PUCKETT CARRIES THE TWINS

"Jump on my back," the star center fielder told his teammates before Game Six in the 1991 World Series and gave a historic performance.

MEMORIES & DREAMS, FALL 2017

Introduction

Twins fans who attended games at the Metrodome from 1984 to 1995 can still hear in their mind's ear the sound of Bob Casey's voice announcing the home team's number three batter: Kiiiiiir—BEEEEEEEEE Puckett! The excitement in his voice mirrored what we felt as fans when we saw the lovable Puck come to bat or chase down fly balls in the outfield—where they went to die in his oversized glove. He was our superstar, and never more so than on an October night in 1991.

It's the stuff legends are made of—the kind of moment that engraves a player's name on a Hall of Fame plaque. On October 26, 1991, with his team on the brink of World Series defeat, Kirby Puckett took it upon himself to win the day with the greatest single-game performance of his career.

The Twins had won the first two games of the 1991 Series at home but then lost three straight in Atlanta, including a 14–5 disaster of Game Five. They returned to Minneapolis with the momentum against them and their confidence in tatters.

After batting practice, the Twins clubhouse in the depths of the Metrodome was quiet. Subdued. Puckett didn't like that. He believed they could still win. He told his teammates not to worry. "Jump on my back," he said. "I'm going to carry us tonight."

It was a bold pronouncement followed by an even bolder performance. The kind only Puckett, it seemed, could make.

"If we needed a big hit or someone to win a game with his glove or his bat, he was the guy who would make those plays for us," says teammate Gene Larkin. "Puck was our leader."

The 31-year-old with the beer keg build and effervescent smile was in the sweet spot of his prime. Six games into a 10-year consecutive All-Star streak, coming off his fifth Gold Glove season, one of the fastest players to reach 1,000 hits in the majors, and on his way to becoming only the second to notch 2,000 in his first 10 full seasons (after George Sisler), Kirby Puckett was the most beloved player in Twins history and the heartbeat of the team.

"I just felt really good that day," he said in an interview several years later.

Puckett had been good before in Game Six. Four years earlier, in 1987, when the Twins won their first World Series, the team had also faced elimination in that game. Down 5–2 in the bottom half of the fifth, Puckett singled to spark a four-run rally. The next inning, he drew a walk and scored on Kent Hrbek's grand slam. He led off the eighth with another hit and scored again, contributing four hits and four runs to the Twins' victory that day.

Now in Game Six of the 1991 Series, batting third, his accustomed spot, Puckett came to bat in the first inning against the Braves with one out and teammate Chuck Knoblauch on first. The ever-eager Puckett laced the second pitch into left for a triple that scored Knoblauch and gave the Twins an early 1–0 lead. He scored himself two batters later.

The Braves looked certain to score in the top of the third with a runner on first and Ron Gant's blast headed for the wall in deep left-center. But Puckett had other plans. The center fielder made a good turn upon contact and raced straight to the wall. He measured several quick stutter steps on the warning track, getting his timing down, and leaped—lifting his 5-foot-8 frame three feet or more off the ground and extending his left arm fully to backhand the ball, robbing Gant and the Braves of an extra-base hit and a run.

Two innings later, Puckett was back at bat, bottom of the fifth, this time with a runner at third and one out. The Braves had tied the score 2–2, in the top half. Eager to put his team back in the lead, Puckett, impatient at the plate, swung at the first pitch and lofted a deep drive to center field for a sacrifice fly that put the Twins up 3–2.

The Braves tied it again before Puckett batted in the eighth with one out. He singled to right and stole second but was stranded there. The score stalled at 3–3, and Game Six headed into extra innings.

Puckett was due to lead off the bottom of the 11th for the Twins. Charlie Leibrandt came in to pitch for the Braves. The left-hander had struck out Puckett twice in Game One. Watching Leibrandt warm up from the on-deck circle, Puckett thought maybe he should bunt then steal second again. Chili Davis, who followed him in the order, could bring him around to score the winning run with a base hit through the infield.

But when he told Davis his plan, his teammate did not approve. "These people didn't come to see you bunt," he said. "Wait for a hanging change and hit it out of here."

It was not like Puckett to wait. Famous for his free-swinging and able to hit pitches from his shoetops to his shoulders, Puckett admitted, "I haven't seen a pitch I didn't like."

But he took the first pitch, a strike low and away. He took the second pitch, high for a ball. He took the third pitch, low and inside.

The 55,155 fans inside the Metrodome were delirious in anticipation. They were not used to seeing this from their beloved hero. He had already played an amazing game: two hits, a stolen base, a run scored, two runs batted in—he had accounted for all three of the Twins runs—and saved at least a run with that spectacular catch. They wanted him to do something, not stand there without swinging the bat. Heroes acted; they took charge.

Leibrandt got the sign. Puckett tapped the far corner of the plate with his black Louisville Slugger, pulled it back, and swirled the top end in little circles. Leibrandt delivered. Here it came. An outside changeup. Puckett kicked up his left leg, the signature beginning of his swing, brought his bat around—and connected.

Twins radio play-by-play man John Gordon narrated on WCCO radio: "Puckett swings"—his voice rose—"and he hits a blast! Deep left-center, way back, way back!"

In one fluid motion, Puckett followed through, dropped his bat, and scampered out of the box. He was thinking double or, if the ball bounced crazily off the Plexiglas, triple. He ran hard.

His teammates leaped off their dugout seats, scrambled up the steps, and followed the trajectory of his hit. They watched. Waited.

When the ball cleared the Plexiglas, the Metrodome crowd roared louder than an airplane taking off. (Seriously. The noise level exceeded 105 decibels.) They flailed their white Homer Hankies. He had done it for them.

"It's gone!" Gordon yelled. "The Twins go to the seventh game. Touch 'em all, Kirby Puckett."

Leibrandt hung his head and walked off the mound.

Puckett slowed his pace and pumped his right fist. "Yeah!" he shouted. "Yeah!"

His teammates gathered at the plate. He ran toward them and disappeared into the bedlam of congratulations to reach home. Tomorrow night they would win Game Seven. They would celebrate with champagne and parades, but not yet. Now, there was just this one man who had told his teammates to climb on his back, and he had carried them out of the abyss to the point where they could see the summit, an easy day's journey from where they stood.

Puckett emerged, his batting helmet in one hand, and raised his left fist to salute the crowd. Their applause filled the night.

Postscript

Not long after Puckett's early retirement in 1996 when his right eye went bad, we started learning about his dark side. He had a long-standing affair. Sexually harassed a female Twins employee. Was accused of groping a woman in a restaurant bathroom (though found not guilty in court). Threatened his wife with a handgun. Got really fat. Then died suddenly of a stroke in 2006, eight days shy of his 46th birthday. All of that shook us who had loved him for what he'd done on the field. And yet, regardless of his demons and misdeeds, we still had the memory of the way he made us feel in 1991 with his performance in Game Six.

A FALL CLASSIC COMEDY

The Detroit Tigers and Chicago Cubs turned Game Six of the 1945 World Series into a game to remember for all the wrong reasons.

SABR MAGAZINE, SUMMER 2015

Introduction

I wrote this article for the SABR magazine to be published in conjunction with the 2015 SABR Conference to be held in Chicago at the Palmer House. You'll see the connection.

Through five games of the 1945 World Series, the Detroit Tigers held a three-games-to-two lead over the Chicago Cubs. This fall classic was, as *Baseball Magazine*'s Clifford Bloodgood called it, "A comedy of errors—loosely played but good entertainment." The comedy continued in Game Six, played at Wrigley Field, though not everyone would find humor in the errors.

A year earlier, Captain Hank Greenberg of the Army Air Forces had been stationed in India, listening to the Series on the radio and figuring he would never play in another one himself. His first three had not been fully satisfying. In 1934, despite putting up decent numbers, he had been criticized for failing to come through in the clutch when the Tigers lost to the Cardinals; Dizzy Dean had mocked him with three strikeouts in Game Seven. The next year, he had injured his wrist and been forced to the sidelines of the team's victory. In 1940, his last full season, he had endured another disappointing seven-game defeat, this time at the hands of Cincinnati.

Now, the Tigers' left fielder had another chance—not only to play, but also to set right his World Series record. It would be his last chance.

In the bottom of the sixth inning of Game Six, Greenberg chased Mickey Livingston's popup blowing back toward the infield. He managed to get his glove on it but couldn't make the catch. The ball fell for a double (the official scorers charitably awarded Livingston a hit), and Livingston later scored to put the Cubs up 5–1.

In the seventh, Greenberg scored, as did teammate Doc Cramer, to trim the Cubs' lead to 5–3. The score would have been 5–4 if not for the Hostetler flop. Chuck Hostetler, at 42 the Tigers' fastest runner, had rounded third on Cramer's single hell-bent on home when his toe caught the turf. He stumbled, lurched forward several strides windmilling his arms, then belly-flopped into no-man's-land. Instead of scoring, he was tagged out.

The Cubs increased their lead by two in the bottom half of the seventh, but the Tigers rallied again in the eighth, pulling within a run at 7–6. The day before, Greenberg had pledged to homer in Game Six. Now he faced the gray-haired left-hander Ray Prim with two outs and nobody on. Greenberg worked the count to 3–2 then clubbed the ball. Despite a strong wind blowing in, Greenberg's clout soared over the left-field ivy and tied the game. The Tigers players jumped to their feet, cheered, and danced spontaneously. "That's it!" Tigers manager Steve O'Neill yelled from the third-base coach's box. "That's the payoff." They were certain victory and the championship was theirs.

That is, until Hank Borowy came on in relief and closed the door. With the score tied 7–7, the game headed into extra innings. In the bottom of the 12th, with shadows cramping visibility, Chicago's Stan Hack batted with pinch-runner Bill Schuster on first and two outs. Hack smacked a routine single to left. Greenberg moved in to field it, wanting to nip the runner at third to finish off the Cubs. He dropped to his right knee to play the bounce, but the ball struck a sprinkler head and hopped over his shoulder. Greenberg wheeled and chased the ball to the wall, but Schuster scored standing up. The three official scorers, led by Harry Salsinger of the *Detroit News*, held Greenberg responsible for the loss: E-7.

While the Wrigley Field crowd whooped and hollered, Greenberg made the long, lonely walk from left field to the Tigers clubhouse entrance on the first-base side with his head down, growing angrier by the step. Instead of celebrating a World Series victory—once again the Tigers had squandered a 3–2 series lead—he lamented an extra-inning loss pinned on him, the bum. He stomped into the clubhouse, where his teammates gave him a wide berth. When a reporter asked, "What happened to you on that play, Hank?" Greenberg snapped, "What happened to *me*? What happened to *you*?! Did you see the game?"

Always sensitive to criticism about his limitations in the field, Greenberg was incensed that the scorers had charged him with an error on a ball he didn't think he had a legitimate chance to field. It had bounced over his shoulder! He never touched it. Still, he was down on himself that he had let it get by.

Greenberg's teammates agreed that he had been unfairly accused of misplaying the ball. "How in the hell could anyone give an error on such a play?" O'Neill demanded.

The second-guessing extended beyond the Tigers clubhouse. Members of the press argued over the call back at the Palmer House, their Chicago headquarters for the Series. Some of them finally wore down Salsinger and the other two scorers, who reversed their decision—the first time that had ever happened in the World Series—and awarded Hack a double and an RBI. Greenberg was off the hook but not pleased. He had hit his second home run of the Series, as predicted, but that no longer mattered. The Tigers had lost. The scorers wouldn't change that fact.

Greenberg wouldn't have to mope for long. Two days later, he drew two walks and added a sacrifice fly and a sacrifice bunt, to help the Tigers win Game Seven 9–3 and put them on top once again as world champions.

Postscript

I adapted this article from my biography *Hank Greenberg: The Hero of Heroes*.

SANDY KOUFAX'S YOM KIPPUR DECISION

"The Left Arm of God" famously sat out Game One of the 1965 World Series. What really happened that day in Bloomington?

SPORTS ILLUSTRATED, SEPTEMBER 2015

Introduction

Sometimes it's hard to tell which is better, the true story or the folklore. In the case of Sandy Koufax, they're both good.

On October 7, 1965, the day after the Minnesota Twins had defeated the Los Angeles Dodgers in the first game of the World Series, a 28-year-old Hasidic rabbi named Moshe Feller approached the desk clerk at the St. Paul Hotel and told him he wanted to speak with Sandy Koufax.

The clerk considered the bearded man in the black hat and sidelocks before him. Like everyone else, he knew that Koufax had not pitched Game One because it fell on Yom Kippur, and he must have figured this man was the pitcher's rabbi. He gave him Koufax's room phone number.

Koufax answered. Rabbi Feller told him what he had done was remarkable, putting religion before his career, and that as a result more people had not gone to work and more children had not gone to school to observe the Day of Atonement. He said he wanted to present Koufax with a pair of tefillin, scrolls of scripture worn by Jewish men during weekday prayers.

Koufax invited the rabbi up to his room on the eighth floor.

In Rabbi Feller's account, he told Koufax he was proud of him for "the greatest act of dedication to our Jewish values that had even been done publicly" and presented him with the tefillin, which he said Koufax took out of their velvet box and handled reverently.

Whether or not such a meeting actually occurred, Rabbi Feller's story speaks to the powerful impact Koufax's decision had on American Jews—then and now, 50 years later. "It's something that's engraved on every Jew's mind," says Rabbi Feller, now 78. "More Jews know Sandy Koufax than Abraham, Isaac, and Jacob."

Yet there remains mystery to the story. The few times that Koufax has explained his decision not to pitch that first game of the 1965 Series, he has claimed it was routine, that he always observed the High Holy Days by not pitching. In his eponymous autobiography published the following year, he writes, "There was never any decision to make . . . because there was never any possibility that I would pitch. Yom Kippur is the holiest day of the Jewish religion. The club knows I don't work that day."

In the 2010 documentary film *Jews and Baseball: An American Love Story*, he said, "I had taken Yom Kippur off for ten years. It was just something I'd always done with respect." He repeated that rationale in a 2014 interview with the *Jewish Week*.

But it's not that neat and simple. In 1960, Koufax pitched two innings of scoreless relief on October 1, the day of Yom Kippur, not long after the holiday ended at sundown in an otherwise unmemorable loss with the Dodgers 13 games out of first place. The following year, Koufax started the Dodgers' September 20, 1961, game mere minutes after sundown ended Yom Kippur and turned in a 13-inning winning performance, even though his team was again out of contention. Both games he showed up at work before the holiday—and its restrictions—ended.

When he announced his intention not to pitch Game One the week before the 1965 Series, Koufax said he had not suited up for World Series games in the past when they fell on Yom Kippur. But that had not happened either. In the four years that the Dodgers appeared in the World Series when Koufax was part of the team (1955, 1956, 1959, and 1963), Yom Kippur had never fallen on a game day.

So why, this time, did he defer to his religion, when he hadn't in the past?

Most likely because the circumstances had changed. The Sandy Koufax four and five years earlier was not the Sandy Koufax of 1965. During the first six years of his career (1955–60), he had been only mediocre, losing more games than he won, and could show up at the ballpark on the High Holy Days without attracting much attention or causing any controversy.

But after he learned not to try to throw as hard as he could—which actually gave his fastball more movement—and made some mechanical adjustments, that changed. From 1961 to 1965 Koufax went 102–38, posted the National League's lowest ERA the last four seasons, and pitched four no-hitters, including a perfect game in September 1965. The 1965 season had been the best of his career: he led the majors with 26 wins and a 2.04 ERA while shattering Bob Feller's single-season strikeout record of 348 with 382 of his own, on his way to another Cy Young Award. He had become "The Left Arm of God."

Koufax knew what that meant. Even though he was a secular Jew, he had been raised in the Jewish neighborhood of Bensonhurst and been signed in 1954 by the then-Brooklyn Dodgers on the strength of being from Brooklyn and Jewish. He no doubt understood that for him as the marquee star to pitch the first game of the World Series on Yom Kippur would be a blow to his people, a very public repudiation of their traditions. More would be lost—even if he won the game—than gained.

It helped, of course, that he had a very competent replacement in Don Drysdale, who had won 23 games that season and two previous World Series starts.

His teammates had not pressured Koufax either way, and several of them told *Sports Illustrated* recently that they had not considered it a big deal even after Drysdale lost Game One and supposedly quipped to Walt Alston when the Dodgers' manager came to lift him in the third inning with the Dodgers trailing 7–1, "I bet you wish I were Jewish, too."

When Koufax deferred to his religious tradition, his teammates stood by him. "Sandy thought it was the right thing to do—it was," says Dick Tracewski, former Dodgers infielder and Koufax's roommate. "Everybody respected that."

When Koufax first announced his decision—on the eve of striking out 13 on two days' rest to clinch the National League pennant—it was a small item in most mainstream newspapers outside of Los Angeles. Dodgers owner Walter O'Malley, a Roman Catholic, even joked to reporters, "I'm going to ask the Pope to see what he can do about rain."

But Koufax's decision was instantly big news among Jews across the country. Michael Paley was a 13-year-old boy living in suburban Boston when he heard the news on the radio that Koufax would not pitch on Yom Kippur. The decision became the talk of his block. "It was the beginning of changed feelings about being Jewish in America," says Paley, now a rabbi and scholar at the Jewish Resource Center of UJA-Federation of New York. "Because of Sandy, we were admired."

Two decades removed from the horrors of the Holocaust and two years before the Six-Day War proved Jewish might, Koufax stood as a symbol of dominance and success. Now he had burnished his reputation as someone willing to honor the traditions of Judaism before all else. His decision meant even more since he was not overtly religious. Had Koufax been Orthodox or regularly attended services, his observance of Yom Kippur would have been expected. But the fact he had shown up on Yom Kippur to pitch in the past and was not religious made his decision in 1965 even more significant.

It bonded secular Jews with the observant and forged a new cultural identity for American Jews. "Koufax's decision says this Jewish piece is a real identity, not just for the Orthodox and the religious people," Rabbi

Paley says. "There is such a thing as American Judaism. We can live in these two cultures. That's the beginning of having a multicultural identity."

The morning of Yom Kippur, the *St. Paul Pioneer Press* reported that Koufax "will attend services today." The rumor spread that he would do so at Temple of Aaron, a conservative synagogue in St. Paul, which was *the* synagogue of the day and the closest to the Dodgers' hotel.

Rabbis throughout the Twin Cities reported that Koufax attended services at their synagogues. Yet none as persistently and convincingly as Rabbi Bernie Raskas, who presided at Temple of Aaron and insisted until his recent death that Koufax had attended the morning services there. "He told me that he brought Koufax in through the side door and sat him in front where almost no one saw him," says David Unowsky, 73, events manager of Subtext Books in St. Paul. "I think if Bernie said it was true, it was probably true. He was an honorable man."

But not everyone believes Rabbi Raskas's account. Steve Shaller, who had just had his bar mitzvah in 1965, remembers waiting outside Temple of Aaron for Koufax to show up before the morning services. "I made my poor father stand out in the drizzle with me to see if he came," says Shaller, now 63 and a real estate investor. "He didn't."

Jeremy Fine, associate rabbi at Temple of Aaron, admits that Rabbi Raskas may have fabricated the story to stir up interest in the synagogue or to inspire Jews about their religion. "I wouldn't put it past him to have made it up," Rabbi Fine says.

That's the conclusion Jane Leavy arrived at in her definitive biography, *Sandy Koufax: A Lefty's Legacy*, published in 2002. She is convinced Koufax did not leave his room at the St. Paul Hotel. "Raskas could not have seen him unless he was the room service waiter at midnight [when Koufax would have broken his fast]," Leavy writes.

The only one who knows for certain, of course, is Koufax, and he's not saying. Famously private, he has never liked to talk about his personal life. As a player, he hid his telephone in the oven so he wouldn't hear it ring when the press called. In retirement, he has rarely granted interviews. He did not give Leavy one for her biography. Nor did he respond to requests for this article.

The fitting climax to Koufax's 1965 World Series story occurred when he came back to pitch Game Seven on two days' rest. He had lost Game Two when the cold, damp weather troubled his arthritic pitching elbow, hampering his control, even though he only gave up one earned run over six innings. With friendlier warm weather in Los Angeles for Game Five, he shut out the Twins on four hits. When the Series stretched to seven games back in Minnesota, Alston summoned the willing Koufax.

Though his curve failed him that day, Koufax relied on his fastball to strike out 10 batters and shut out the strong-hitting Twins for the second straight time (they had been blanked only three times during the entire 162-game regular season). His complete-game victory secured the World Series championship for the Dodgers and seemed to validate God's favor upon him.

In the 50 years since, the story of Sandy in 1965 has been told around dinner tables and in bar mitzvah speeches, impressing each generation that hears it. Boston Red Sox pitcher Craig Breslow first heard the story from his grandparents and later in sermons by his rabbi. "Obviously, as a baseball player, and a Jewish left-handed pitcher, Koufax's story resonated with me," Breslow says. "I admired his courage and his faith."

Some Jewish ballplayers have followed Koufax's example by not playing on the High Holy Days of Rosh Hashanah and Yom Kippur, most notably Shawn Green, who consulted Koufax before deciding to sit out a critical game for the National League West division title race on Yom Kippur when he played for the Dodgers himself in 2001. Others, like Breslow, have found different means to balance the commitment to their teams and their religion. "On a number of occasions I have fasted but made myself available to pitch on Yom Kippur," he says. "I believe there are ways to reconcile one's commitment to his faith and also to his professional responsibilities."

Regardless how Koufax's story is observed and what details of it are true, the fact that he sat out Game One in deference to his religious tradition makes him a fixture of American history. "It's one of the best American Jewish stories we have," Rabbi Paley says. "He didn't see the burden of his identity, he saw the possibility of it."

Postscript

One of my regrets is that I was born too late to appreciate the 1965 World Series. I was only a toddler when the hometown team played a classic Series that I would hear people talk about for years until I finally got to see them play in one—and this time, even better, win it—when I was 23.

INDEX

ABOUT THE AUTHOR

John Rosengren is a member of the Society for American Baseball Research and has a master's degree in creative writing. He is the author of nine other books, notably *Hank Greenberg: The Hero of Heroes*, the definitive biography of the Hall of Fame Jewish baseball player, and the novel *A Clean Heart*, about a young man working in a drug treatment center run by a hard-drinking nun with an MBA. A Pulitzer nominee for his journalism, Rosengren has written articles about baseball and many other subjects for more than 100 publications, including the *Atavist*, the *Atlantic*, the *New Yorker*, *Sports Illustrated*, and the *Washington Post Magazine*. His work has been anthologized alongside that of Maya Angelou, Marlon James, Bill Moyers, George Saunders, and Meg Wolitzer. He earned his master's degree in creative writing at Boston University, where he studied under Leslie Epstein, Theo's father. Rosengren lives in Minneapolis with his wife, their two children, and two golden retrievers.